ALL THE PRETTY FLOWERS

PHOTOGRAPHS BY EIRINI PAJAK

ARIZONA HIGHWAYS

Photographs: EIRINI PAJAK

Editor: KELLY VAUGHN

Designer: BARBARA GLYNN DENNEY

Copy Editor: NOAH AUSTIN

Photo Editor: JEFF KIDA

ISBN: 978-0-9989812-1-5

First printing, 2019. Printed in Canada.

ARIZONA HIGHWAYS

Published by the Book Division of *Arizona Highways* magazine, a monthly publication of the Arizona Department of Transportation, 2039 W. Lewis Avenue, Phoenix, Arizona, 85009.

Telephone: 602-712-2200

Website: www.arizonahighways.com

Publisher: Kelly Mero
Director of Sales and Marketing: Karen Farugia
Editor: Robert Stieve
Senior Editor/Books: Kelly Vaughn
Associate Editor: Noah Austin
Creative Director: Barbara Glynn Denney
Art Director: Keith Whitney
Photography Editor: Jeff Kida
Editorial Administrator: Nikki Kimbel
Production Director: Michael Bianchi
Production Coordinator: Annette Phares

Cover: Photographer Eirini Pajak found this desert globe-mallow (*Sphaeralcea ambigua*) near her home in Florence, Arizona. "Usually, these flowers stay upright, but this one was hanging down," she says. "I'm not sure if it was that way because of the rainstorm, but it's what attracted me to the plant." *24 images stacked*

Back cover: A scarlet monkey-flower (*Erythranthe cardinalis*) harbors a small insect on Mount Lemmon, near Tucson. *32 images stacked*

ARTIST'S STATEMENT

Some of my earliest and fondest memories are of being out in nature with my parents — my father showing me a lizard, or my mother pointing out a dung beetle or the leaves of a sensitive plant. When I was away at college, I went through a difficult time. My uncle, a photographer, heard about it and sent me a letter with several of his nature images enclosed. He wrote encouraging me to get outdoors with a camera and explore. I did, and I began to pay closer attention to my surroundings.

After a while, I set photography aside. Instead, I devoted most of my spare time to learning about the natural world around me. I moved around quite a bit, so knowing the land and living creatures where I lived became a way of making me feel more rooted. When I moved from California to Arizona, one of the first things I did was obtain several nature field guides specific to the state. It wasn't until more than a decade later that I pursued photography again. One day, a monk from St. Anthony's Greek Orthodox Monastery in Florence, Arizona, suggested I begin photographing wildflowers. He emphasized that I should not overlook even the tiniest of flowers. Since then, I've been drawn to making close-up photographs of beautiful, but often overlooked, aspects of nature.

Because of the technique I use, focus-stacking, I often see things in my final images that I didn't even notice with my eyes. I like the idea of the observer's eyes being able to wander around an image the way they could if they were seeing the subject live in nature.

So many sad and chaotic things are going on in the world, and it's easy to get bogged down thinking about them. I find that being outside in nature, exploring and looking for beautiful things, is very therapeutic. I hope my work encourages others to do the same.

— *Eirini Pajak*

Florence, Arizona, 2018

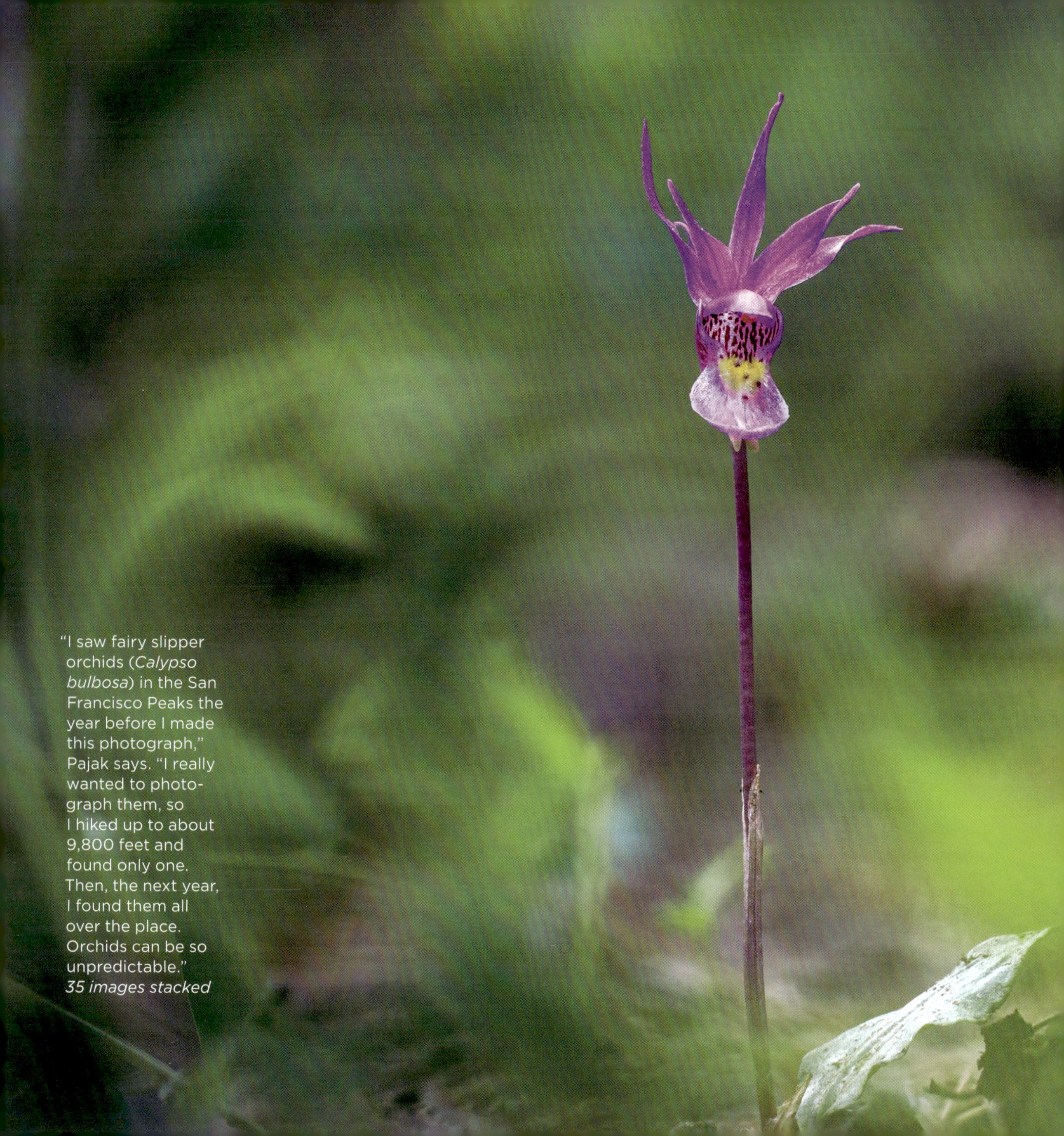

“I saw fairy slipper orchids (*Calypso bulbosa*) in the San Francisco Peaks the year before I made this photograph,” Pajak says. “I really wanted to photograph them, so I hiked up to about 9,800 feet and found only one. Then, the next year, I found them all over the place. Orchids can be so unpredictable.”
35 images stacked

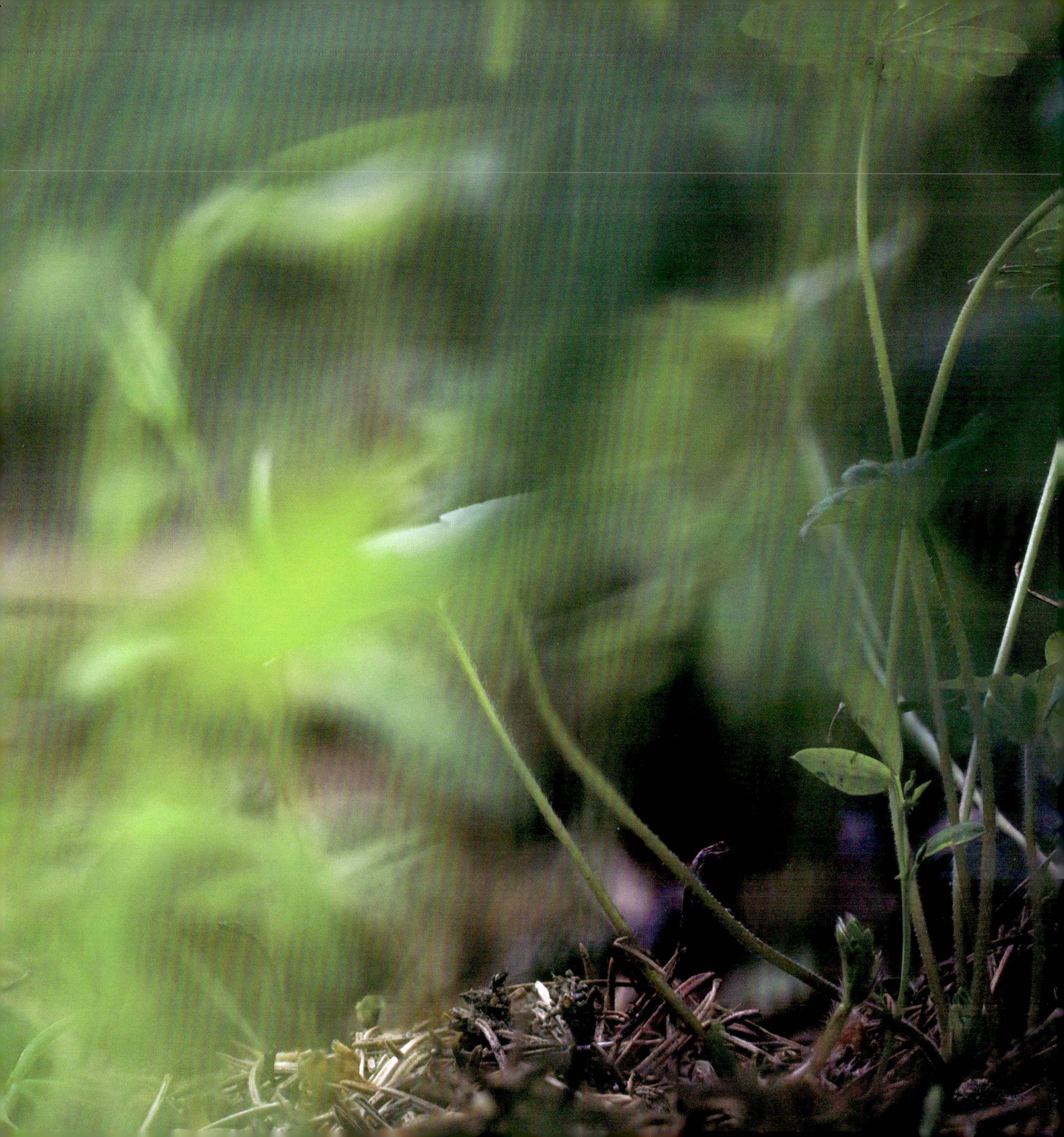

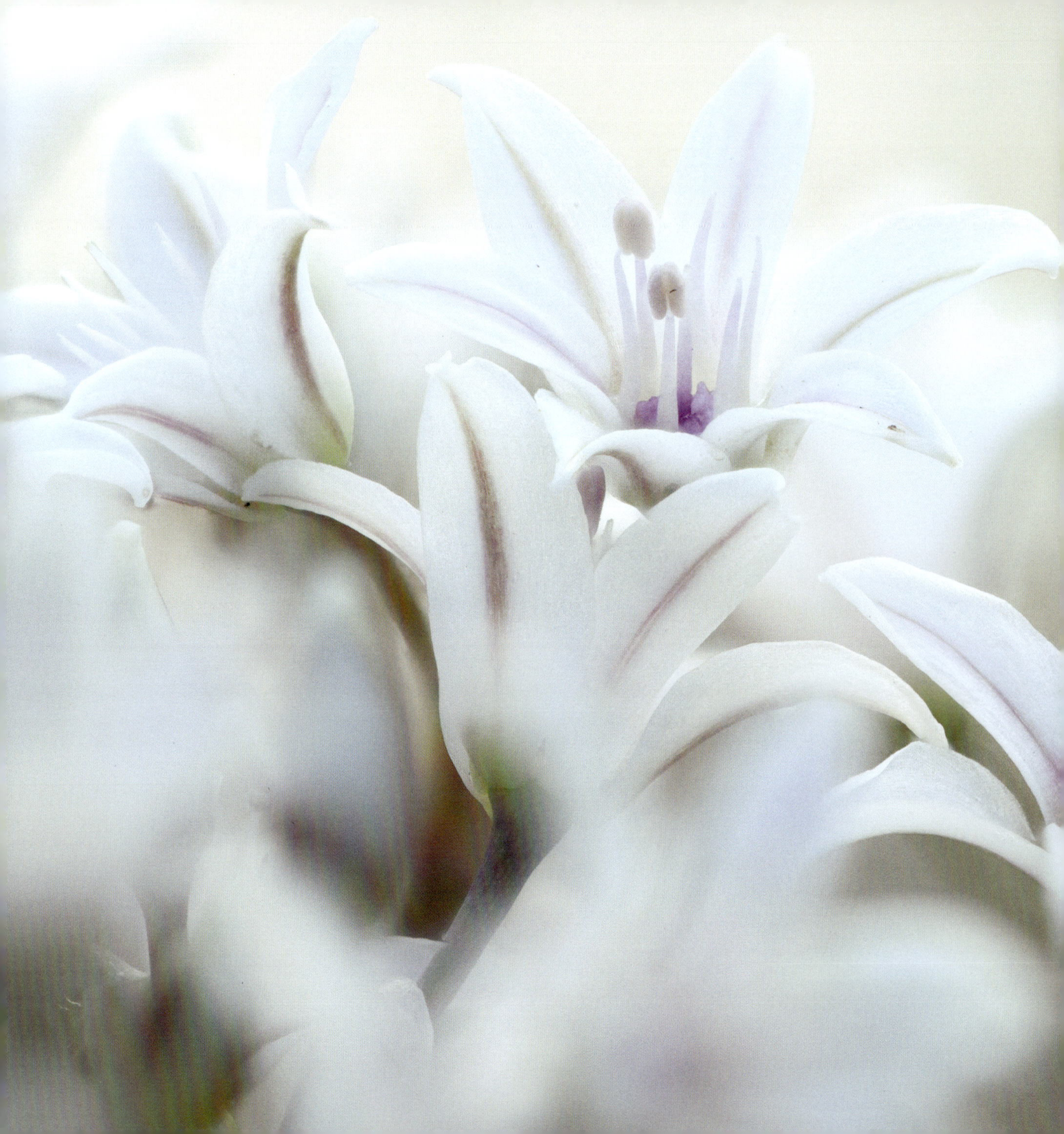

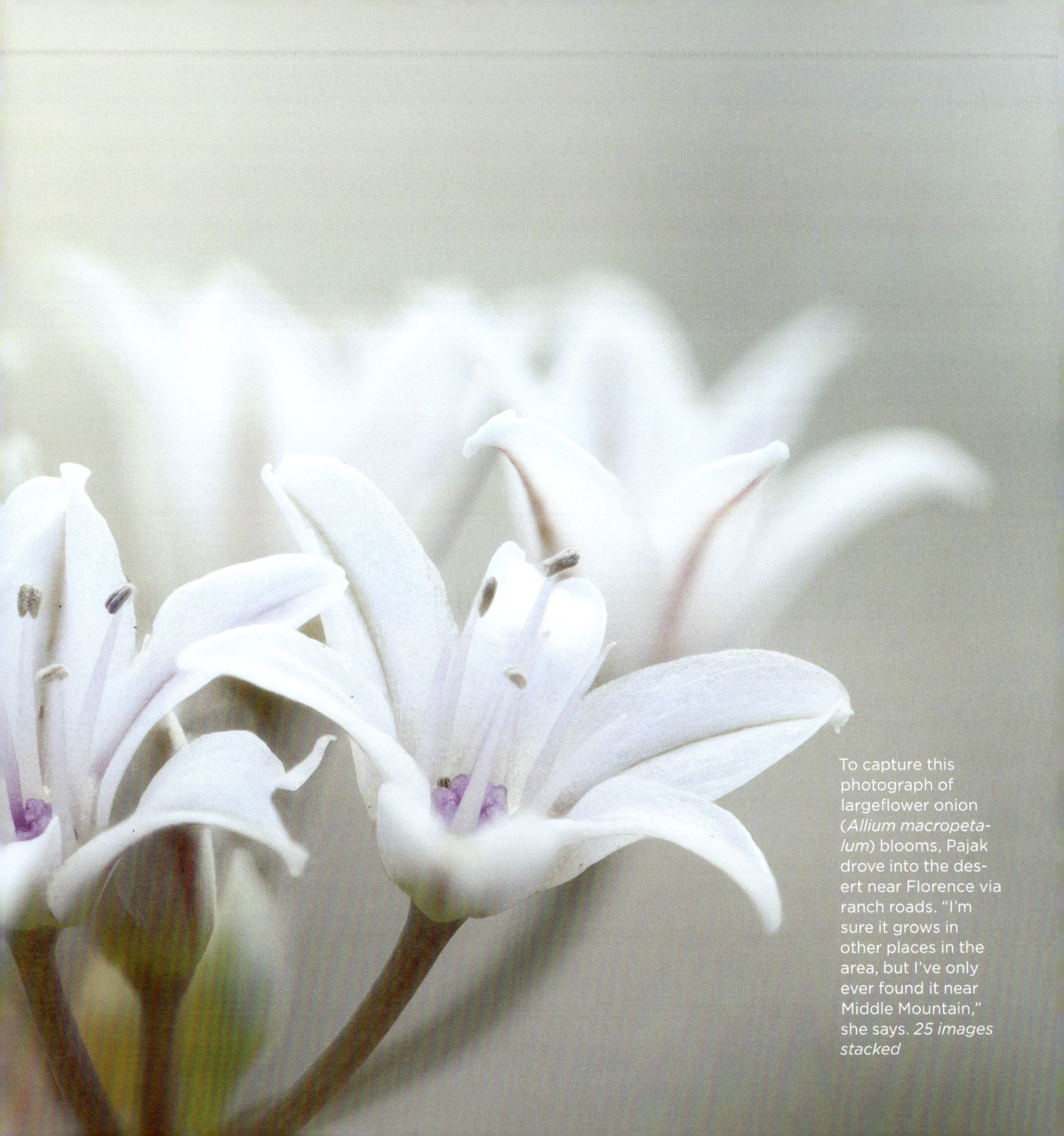

To capture this photograph of largeflower onion (*Allium macropetalum*) blooms, Pajak drove into the desert near Florence via ranch roads. "I'm sure it grows in other places in the area, but I've only ever found it near Middle Mountain," she says. *25 images stacked*

When Pajak traveled to the top of Mount Lemmon to photograph these simple campion (*Silene scouleri*) blooms, her backpack was so heavy, and she spent so much time on the ground, that she had a hard time getting up. "A man came along, very concerned," she says. "I had to reassure him that I was OK." *44 images stacked*

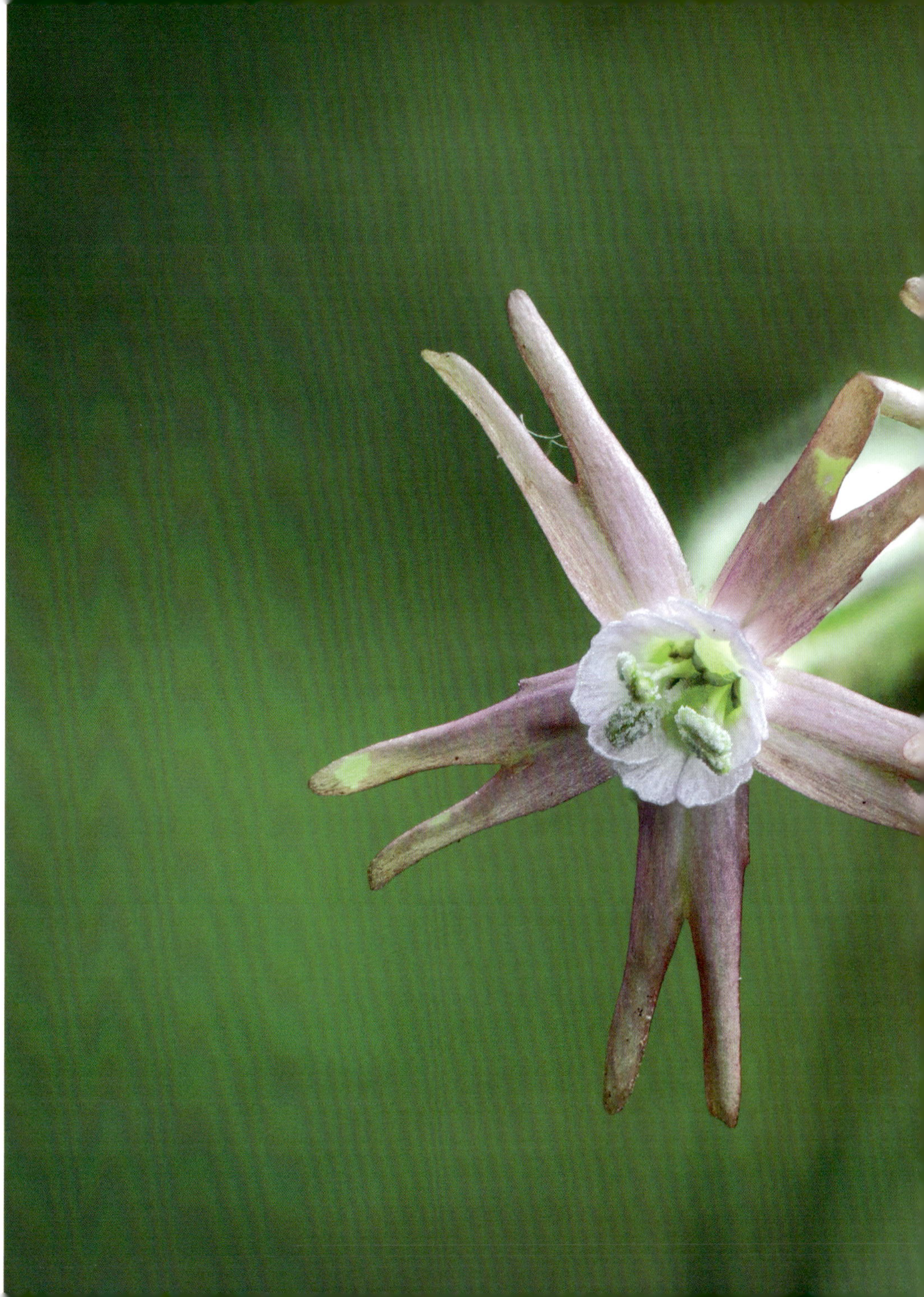

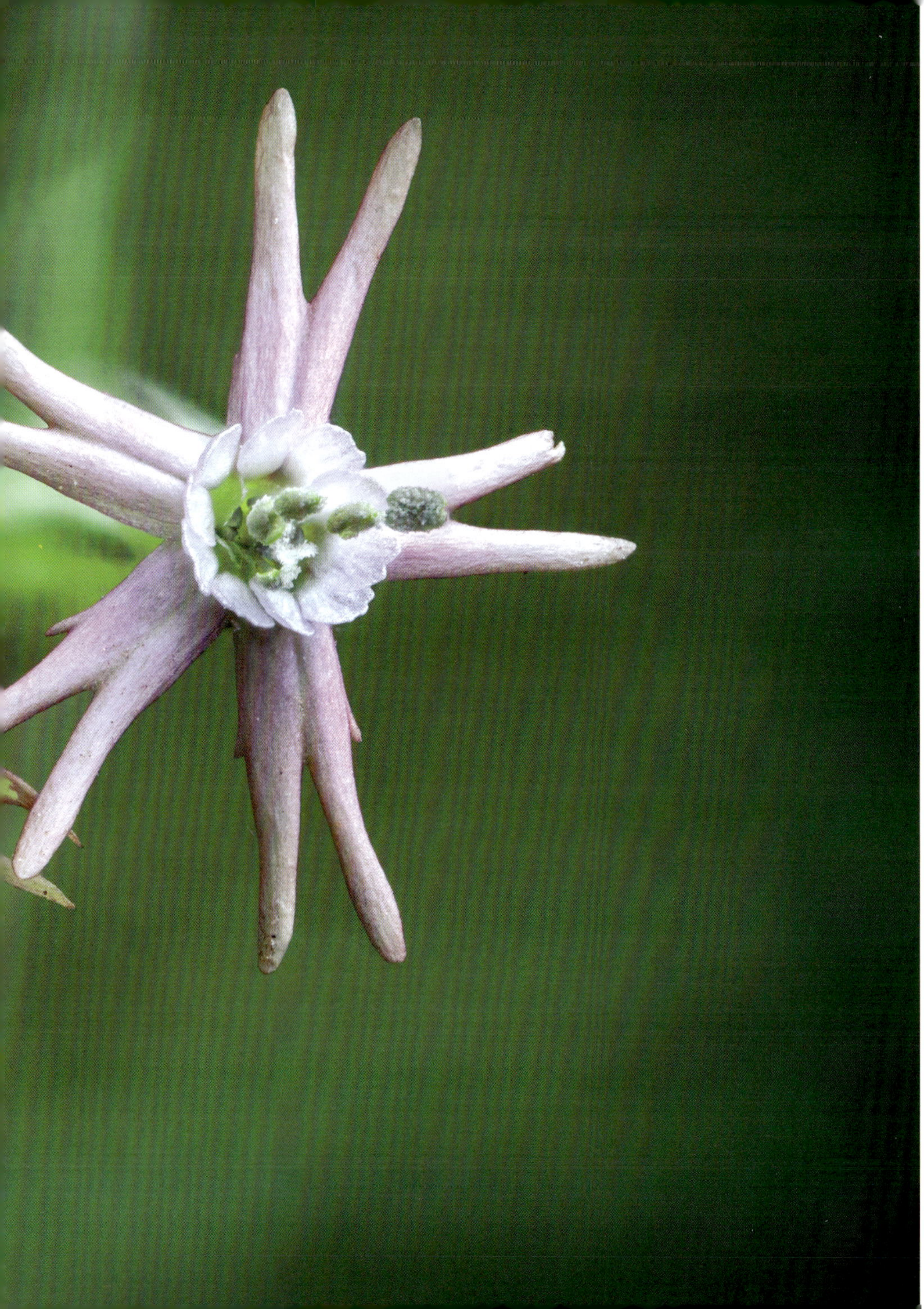

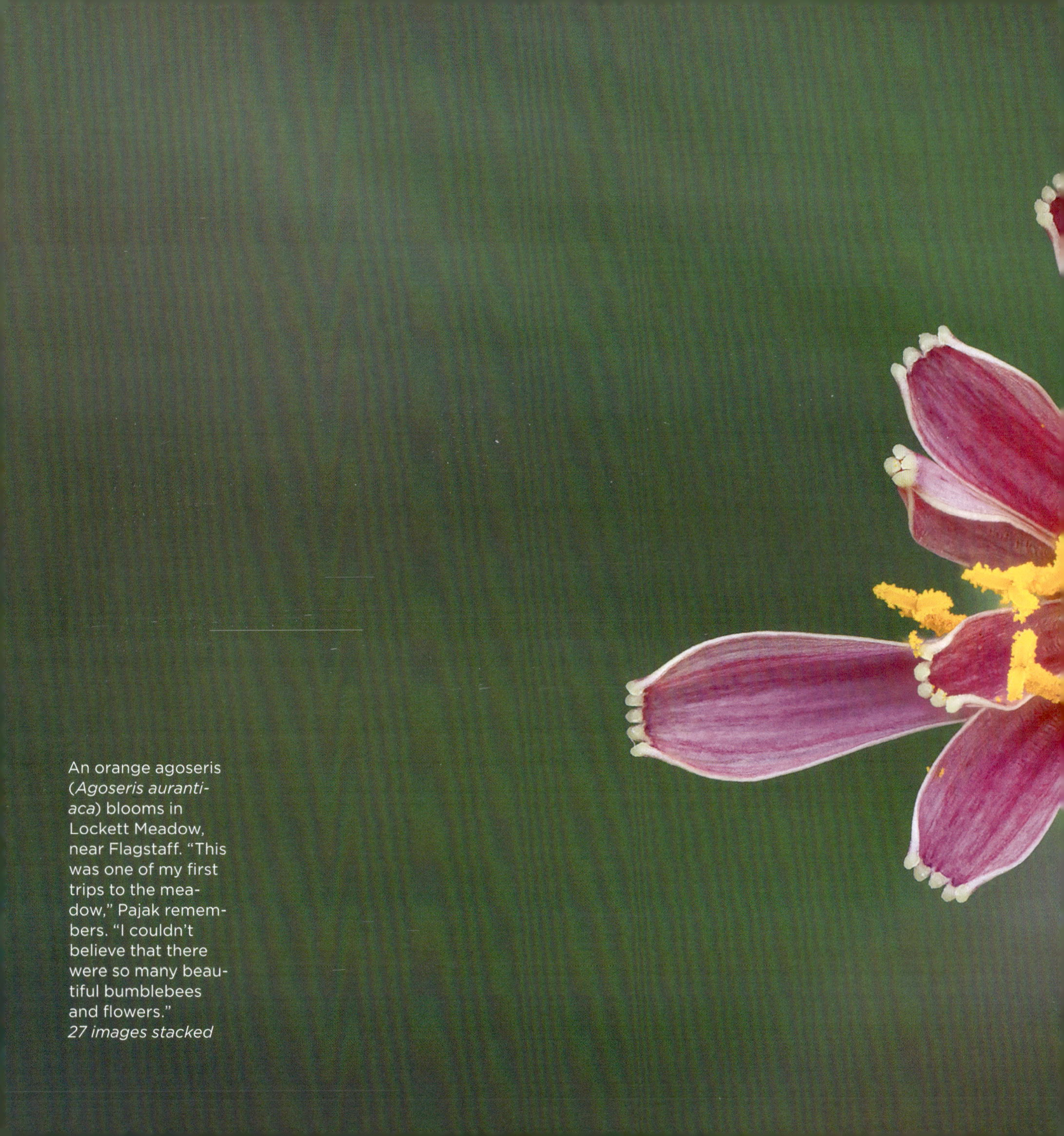

An orange agoseris (*Agoseris aurantiaca*) blooms in Lockett Meadow, near Flagstaff. "This was one of my first trips to the meadow," Pajak remembers. "I couldn't believe that there were so many beautiful bumblebees and flowers."
27 images stacked

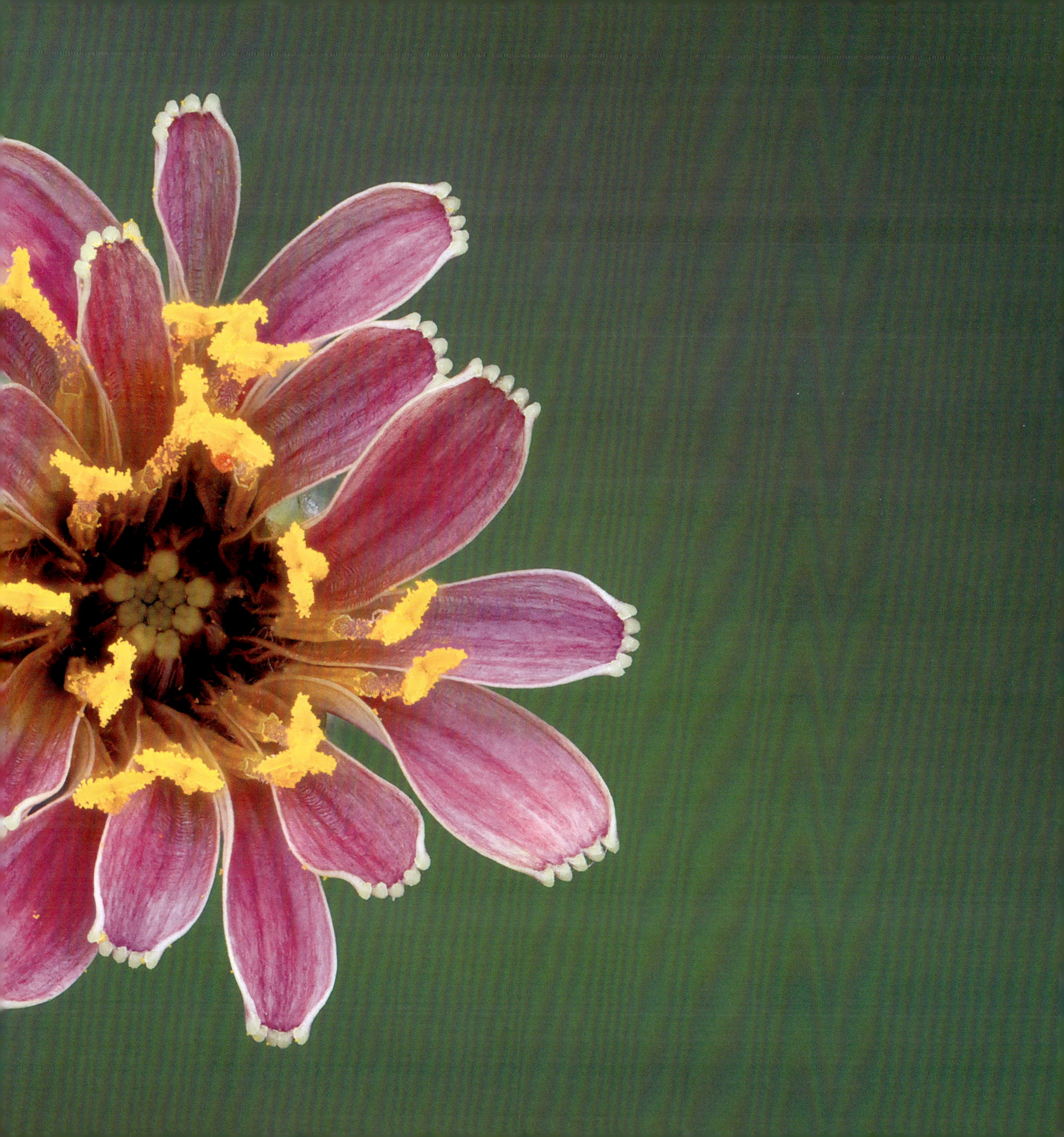

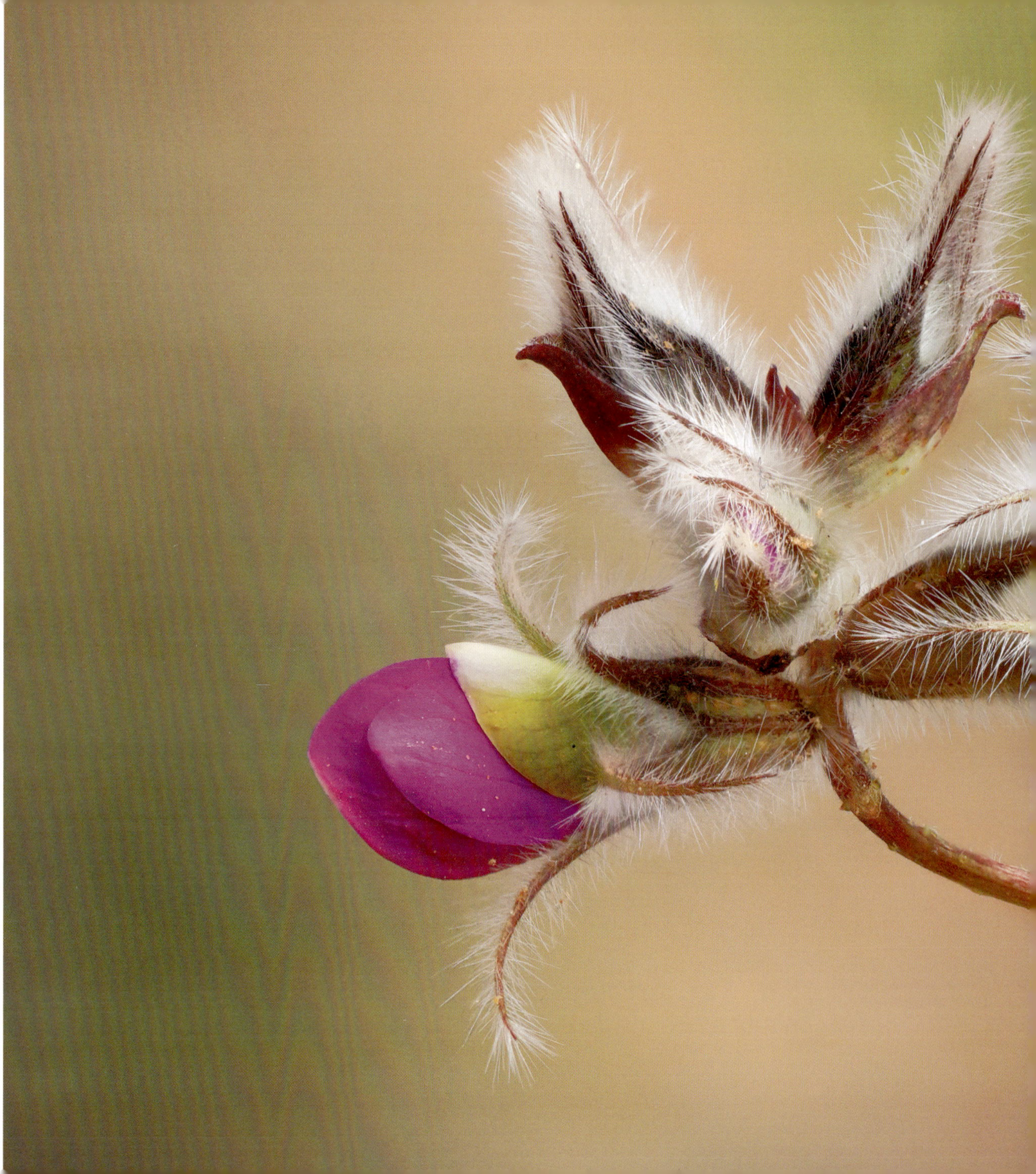

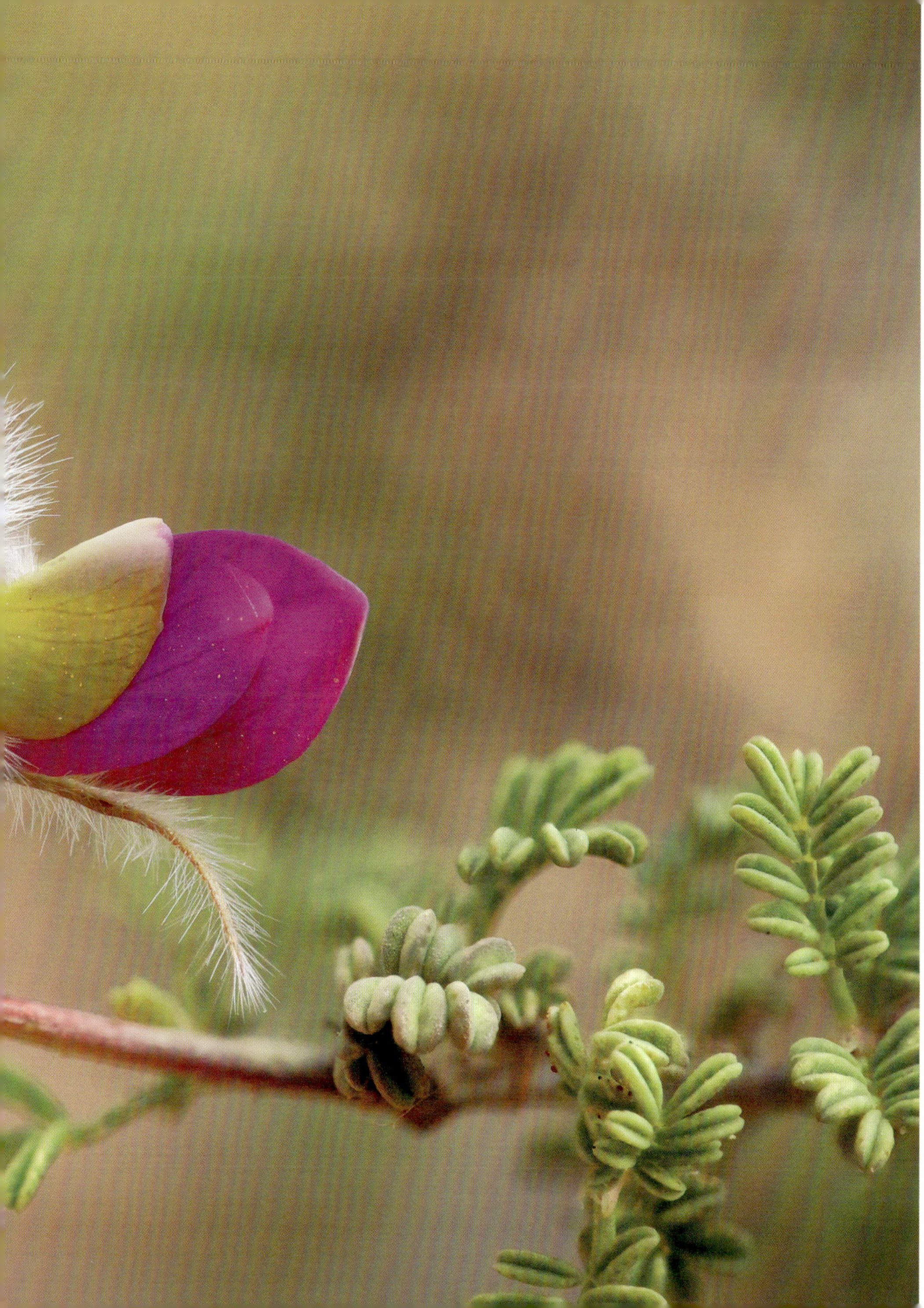

The delicate details of a featherplume (*Dalea formosa*) are revealed in this photograph, made near Bell Rock in Sedona. *45 images stacked*

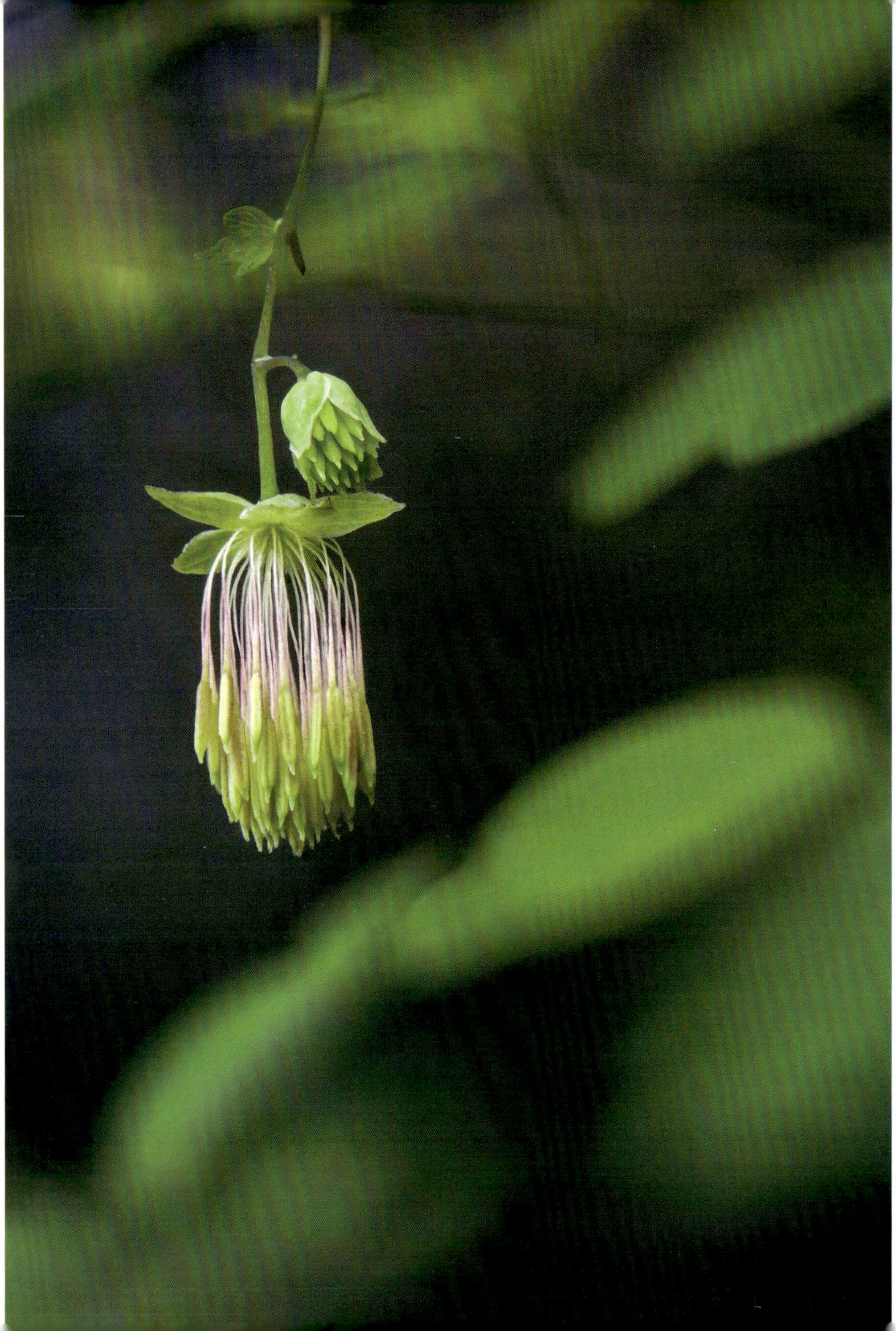

Fendler's meadow-rue (*Thalictrum fendleri*) flowers are so small, they were incredibly hard for Pajak to focus-stack. "Just the slightest breeze would move those little filaments," she says. "It was raining slightly on Mount Lemmon, and for one moment, the air was still, so I kept trying and trying until I got it." *40 images stacked*

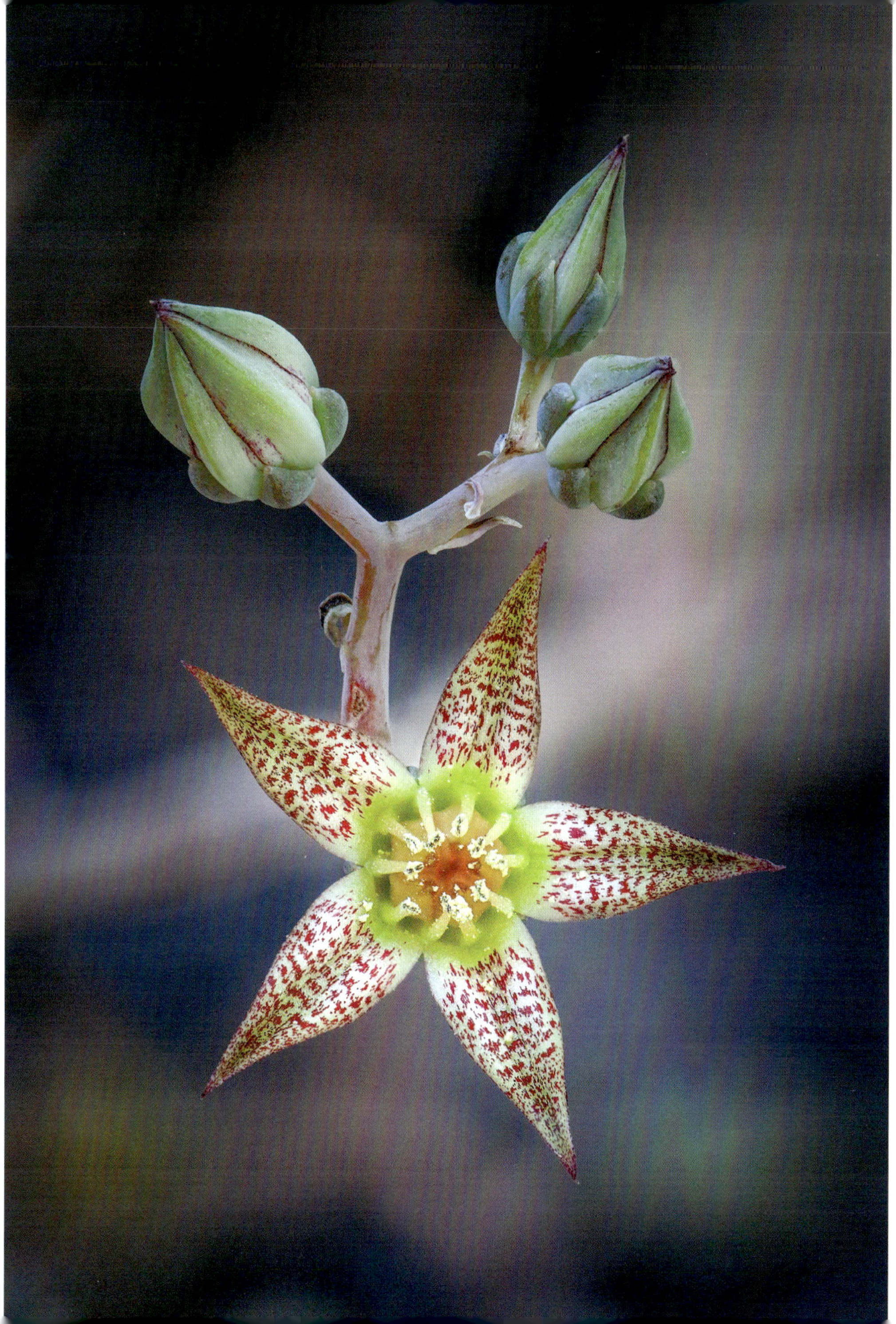

Patagonia Mountain leatherpetal (*Graptopetalum bartramii*) succulents, such as this one in Madera Canyon, southeast of Tucson, are being considered for listing as an endangered species. "People love these little stonecrops, which are endemic to Arizona, so they dig them up and take them home," Pajak says. "It's very sad." *76 images stacked*

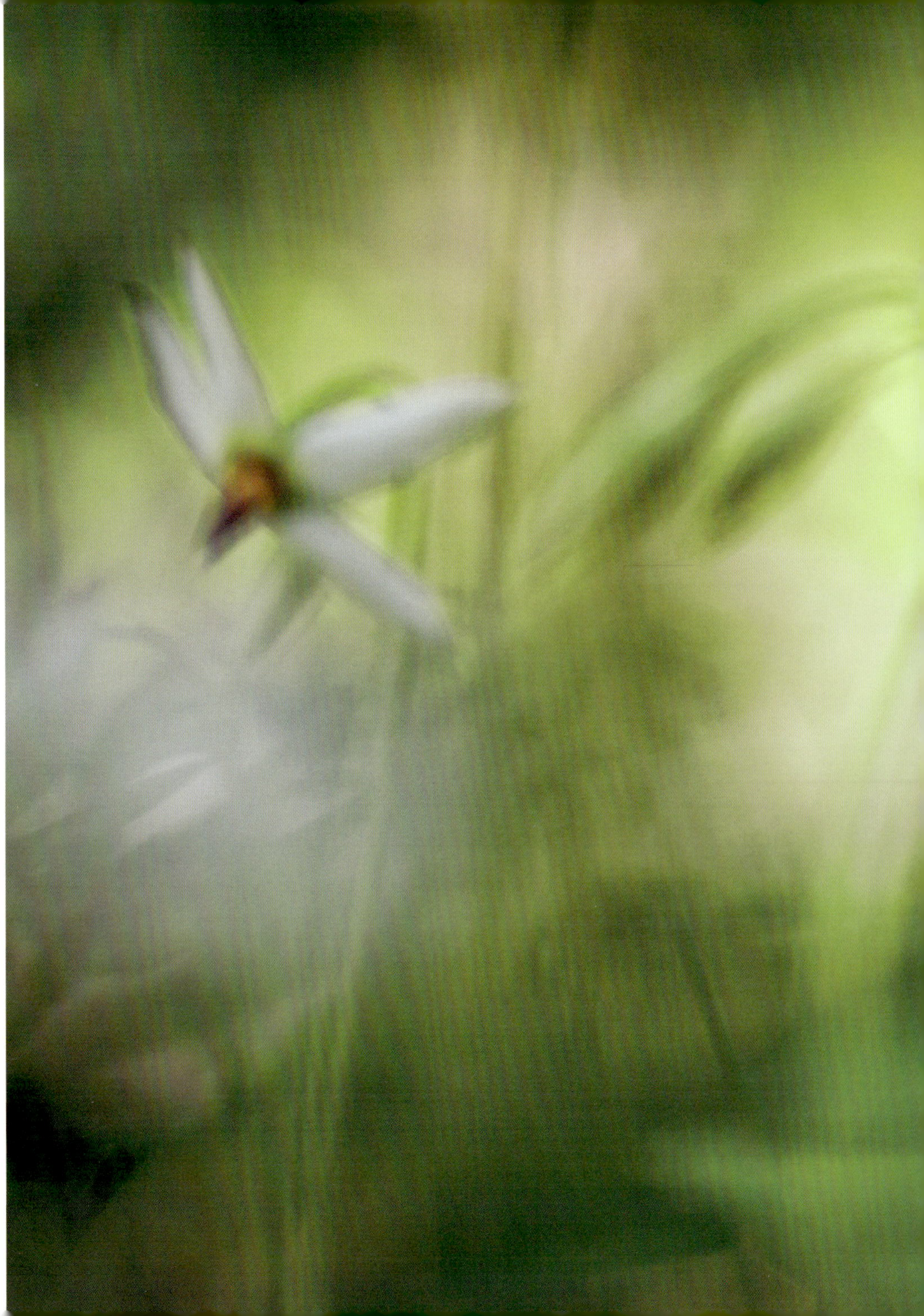

Ellis' shootingstars (*Dodecatheon dentatum ellisiae*), which are endemic to Arizona and New Mexico, emerge from layers of green on Mount Lemmon. *31 images stacked*

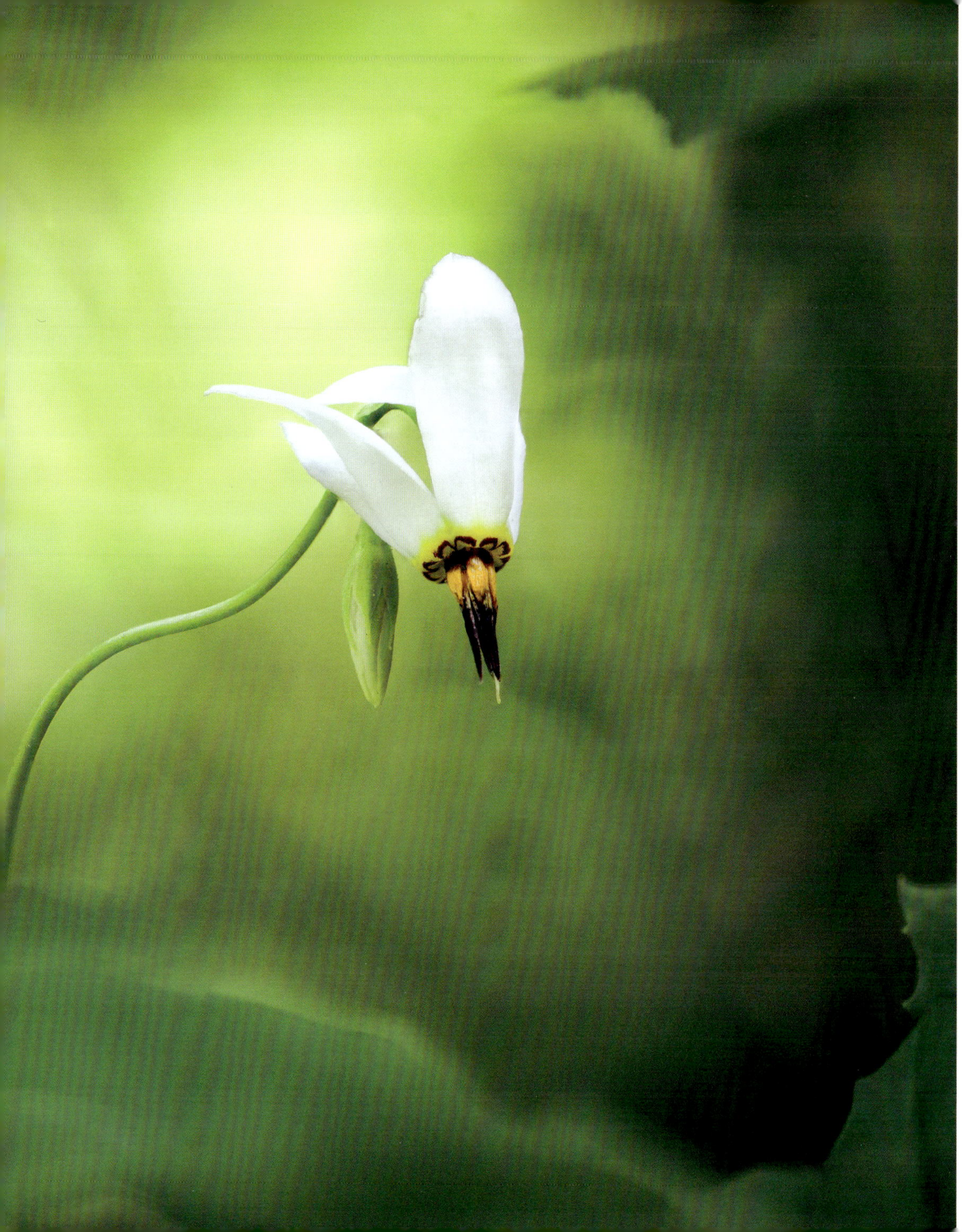

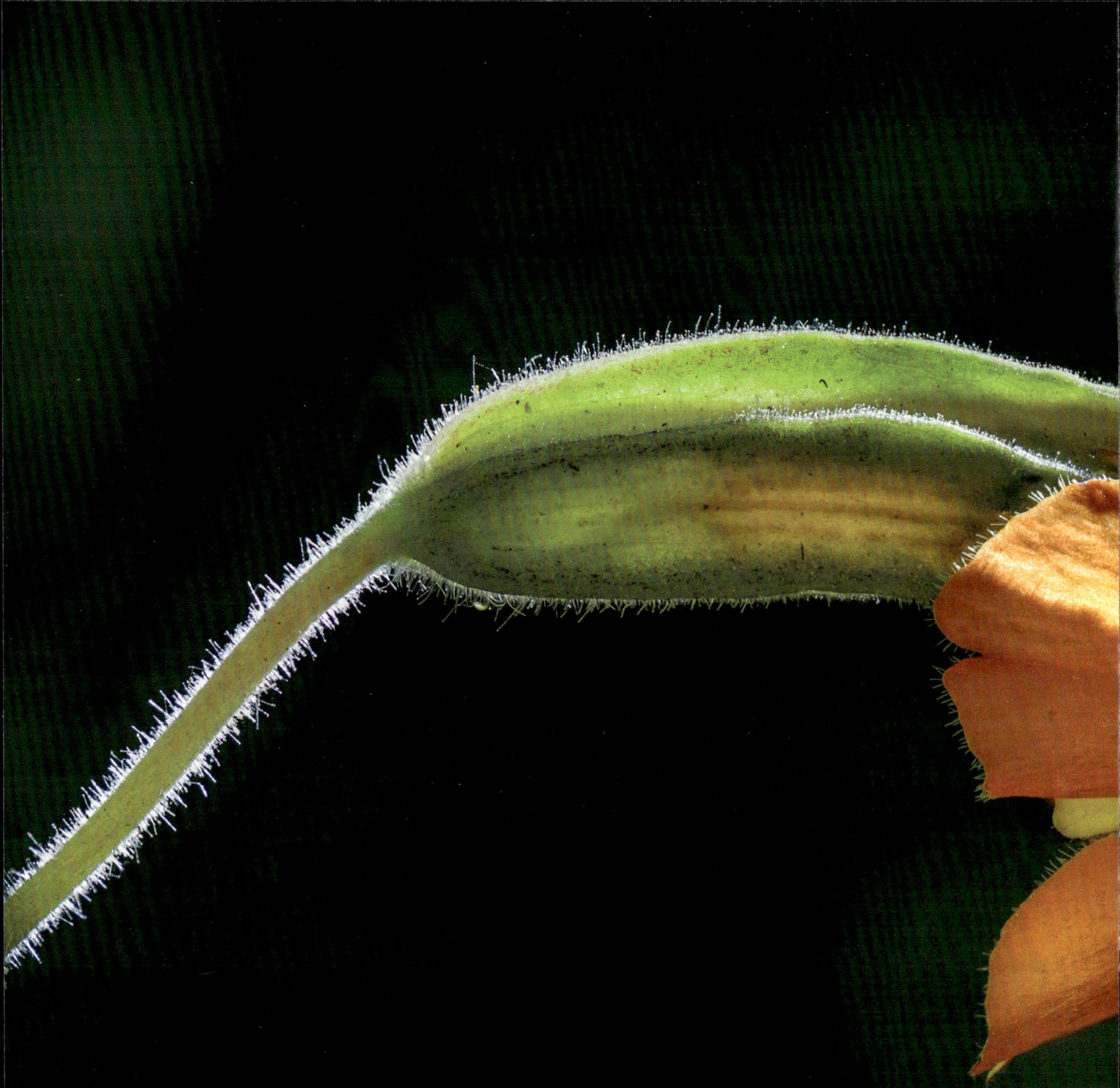

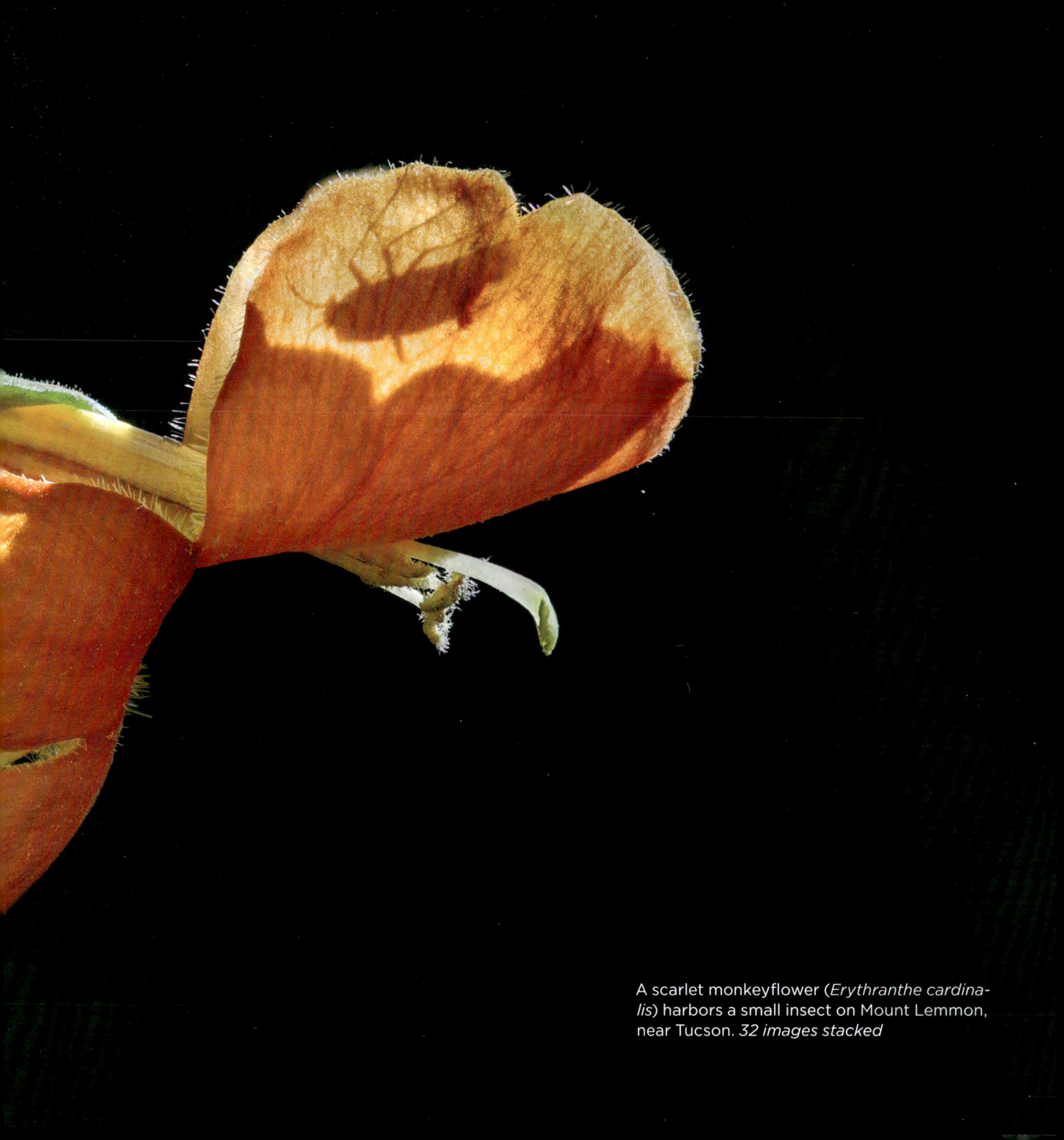

A scarlet monkeyflower (*Erythranthe cardinalis*) harbors a small insect on Mount Lemmon, near Tucson. *32 images stacked*

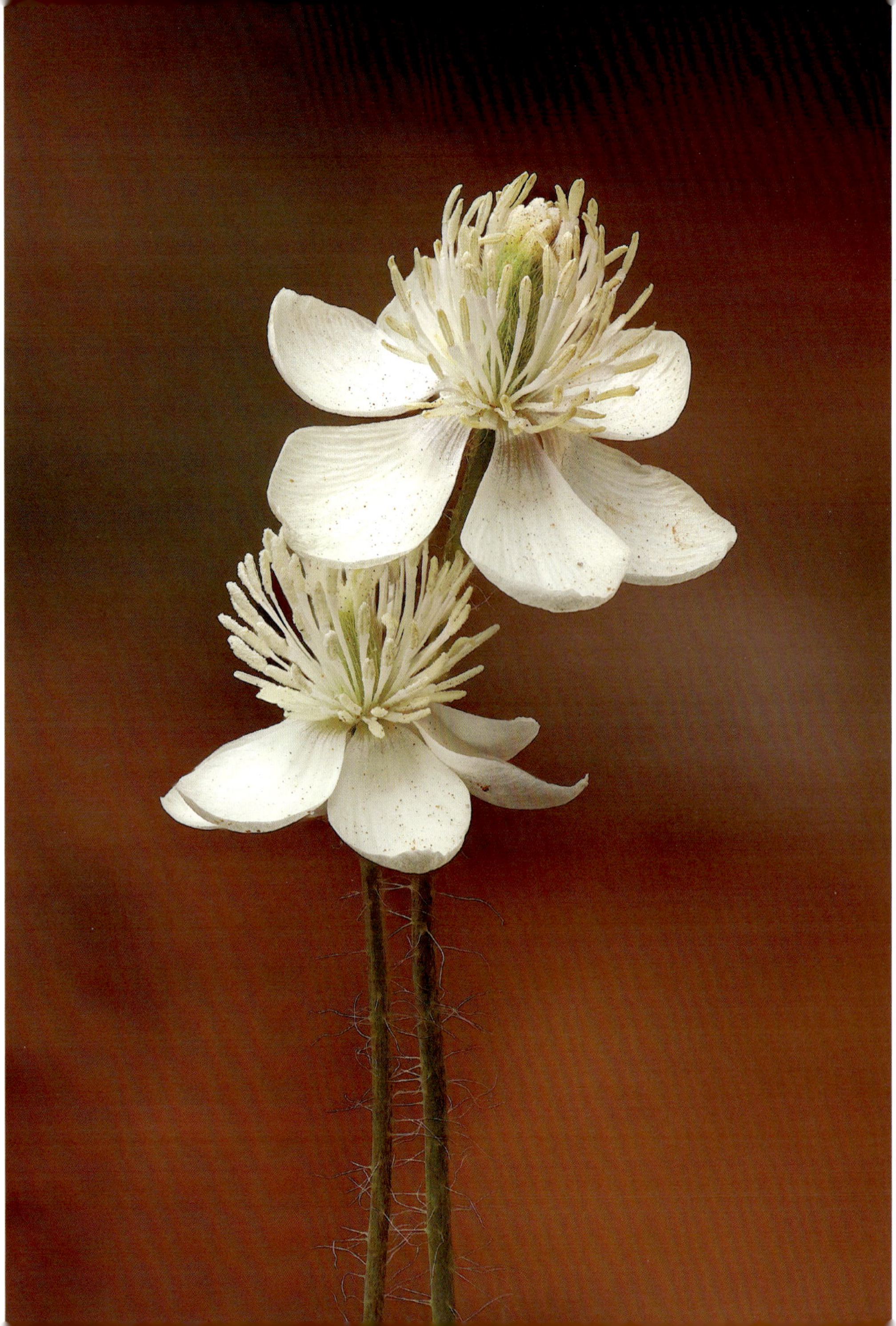

Sedona's red dirt creates an interesting backdrop for creamcup (*Platystemon californicus*) blooms. *77 images stacked*

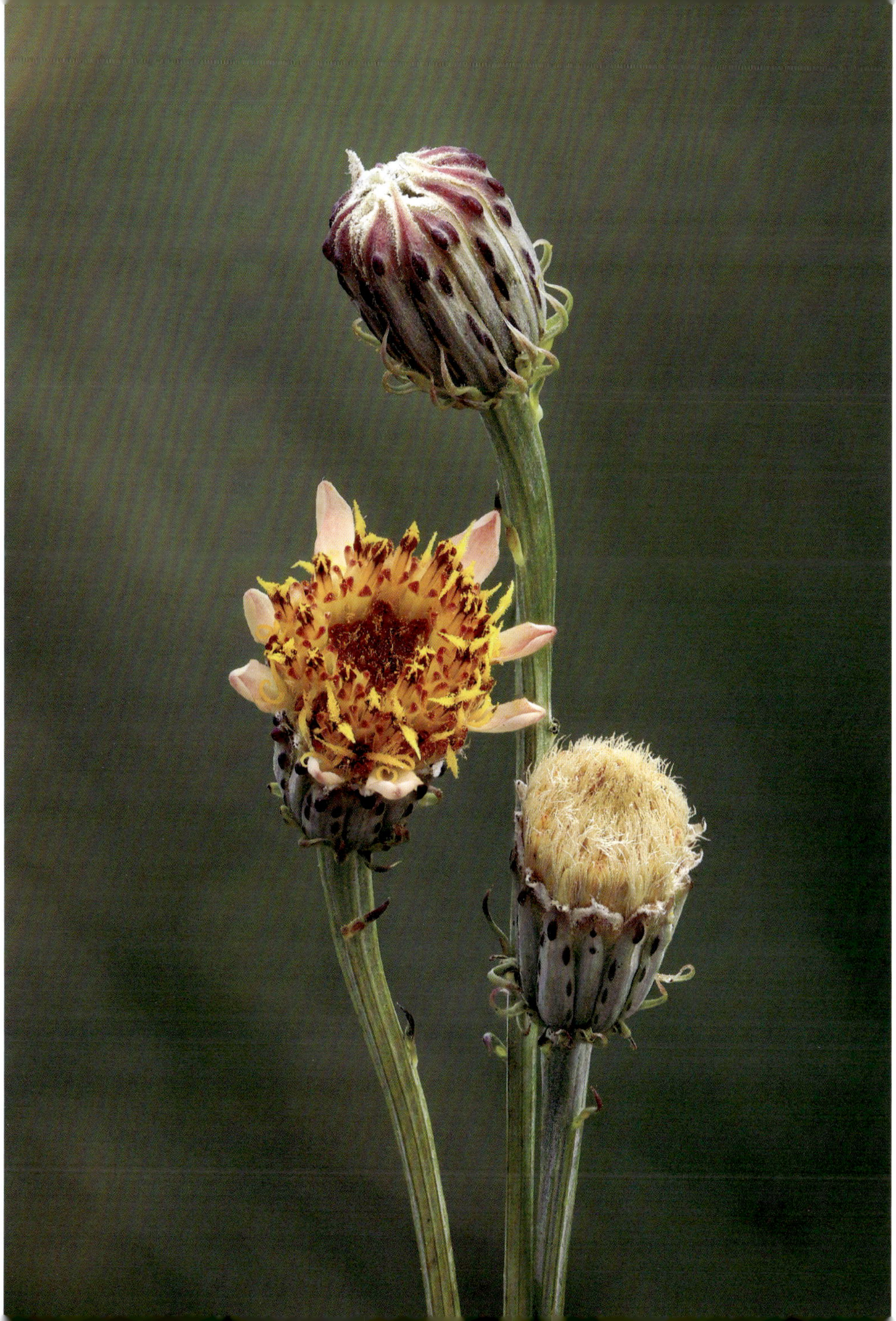

"You really have to look closely at a San Felipe dogweed (*Adenophyllum porophylloides*) flower to realize how pretty it is," Pajak says. "The curves of the little sepals are amazing." She photographed this plant in the desert near her home in Florence. *42 images stacked*

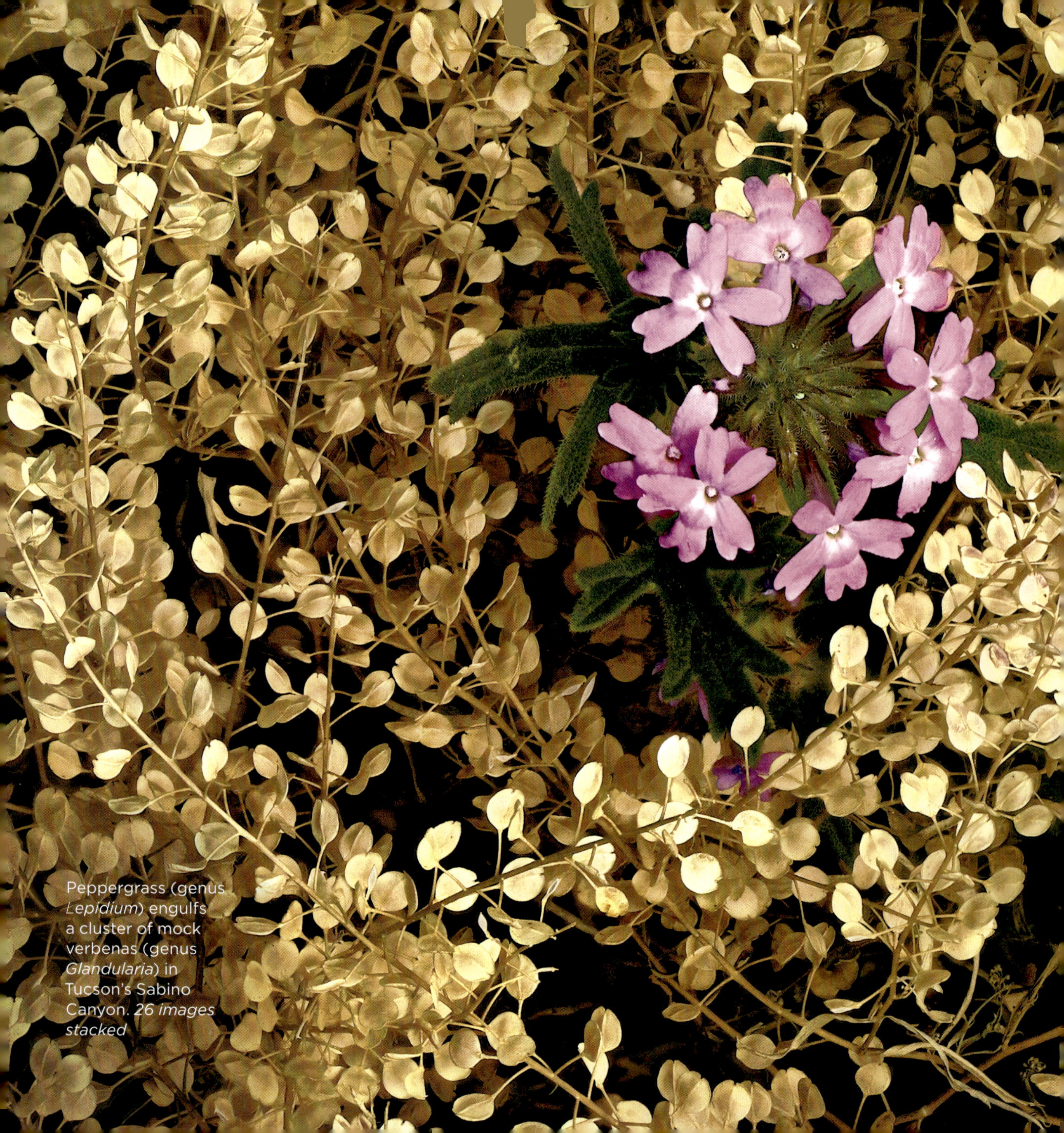

Peppergrass (genus *Lepidium*) engulfs a cluster of mock verbenas (genus *Glandularia*) in Tucson's Sabino Canyon. *26 images stacked*

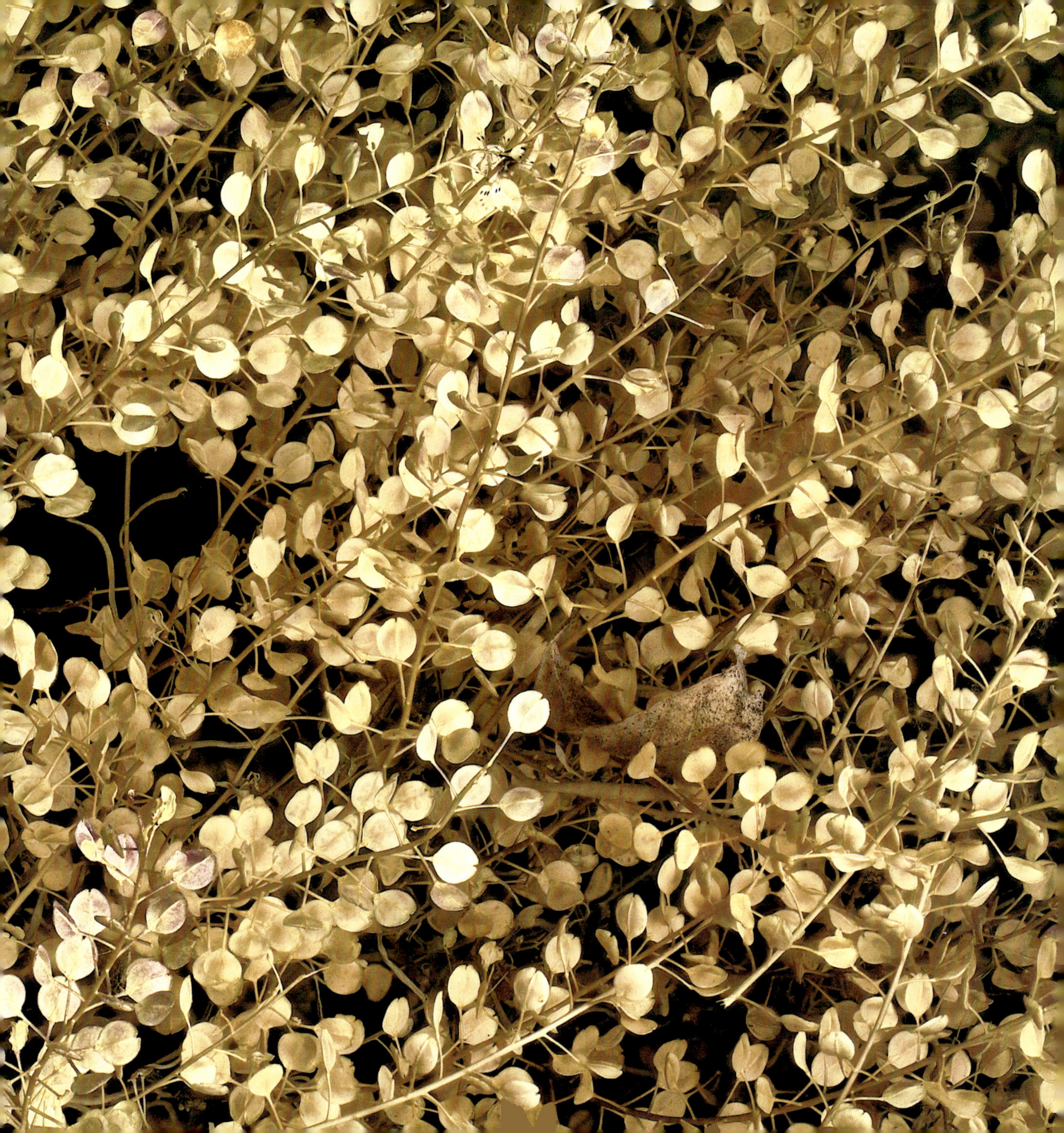

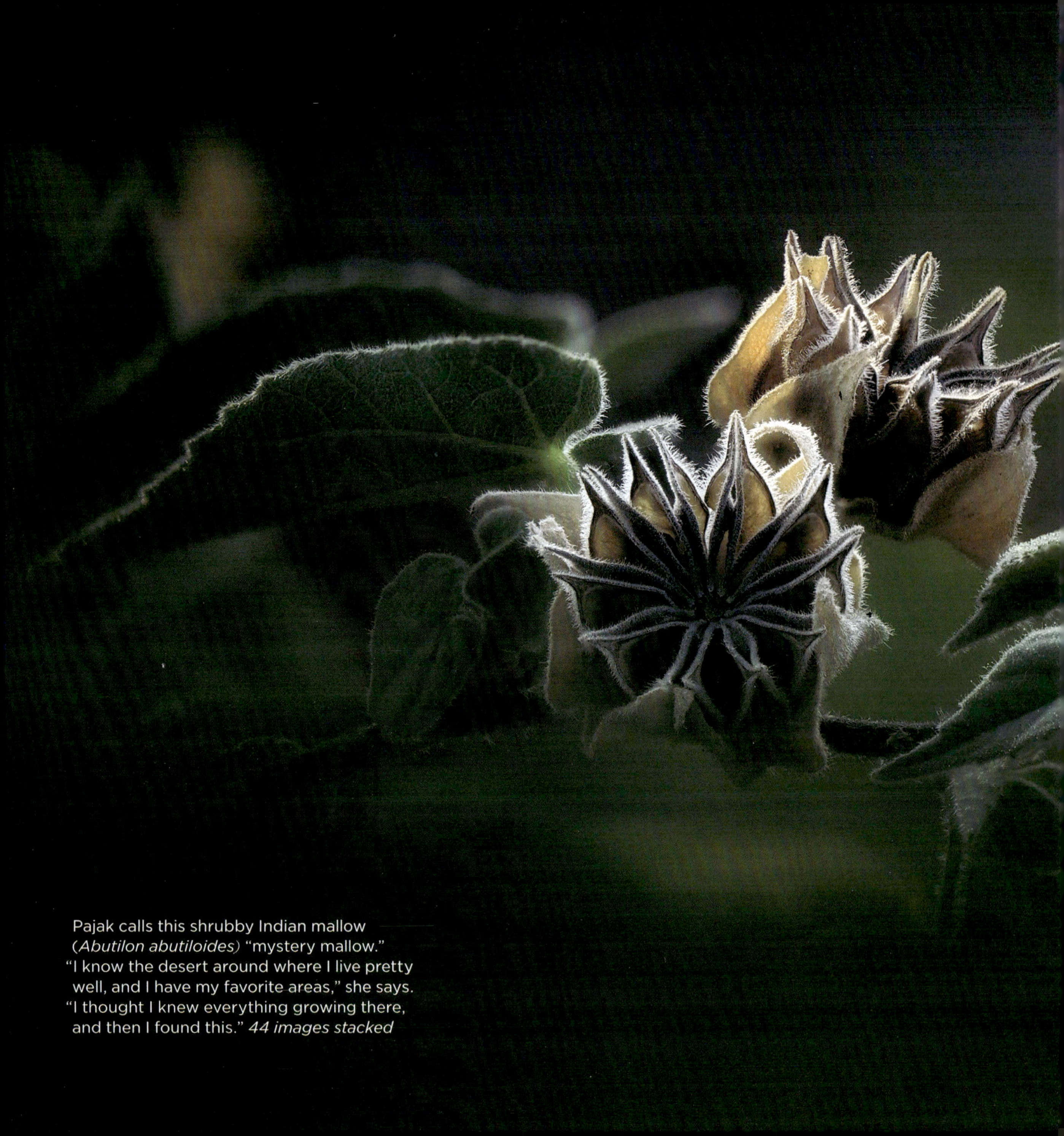

Pajak calls this shrubby Indian mallow (*Abutilon abutiloides*) "mystery mallow." "I know the desert around where I live pretty well, and I have my favorite areas," she says. "I thought I knew everything growing there, and then I found this." *44 images stacked*

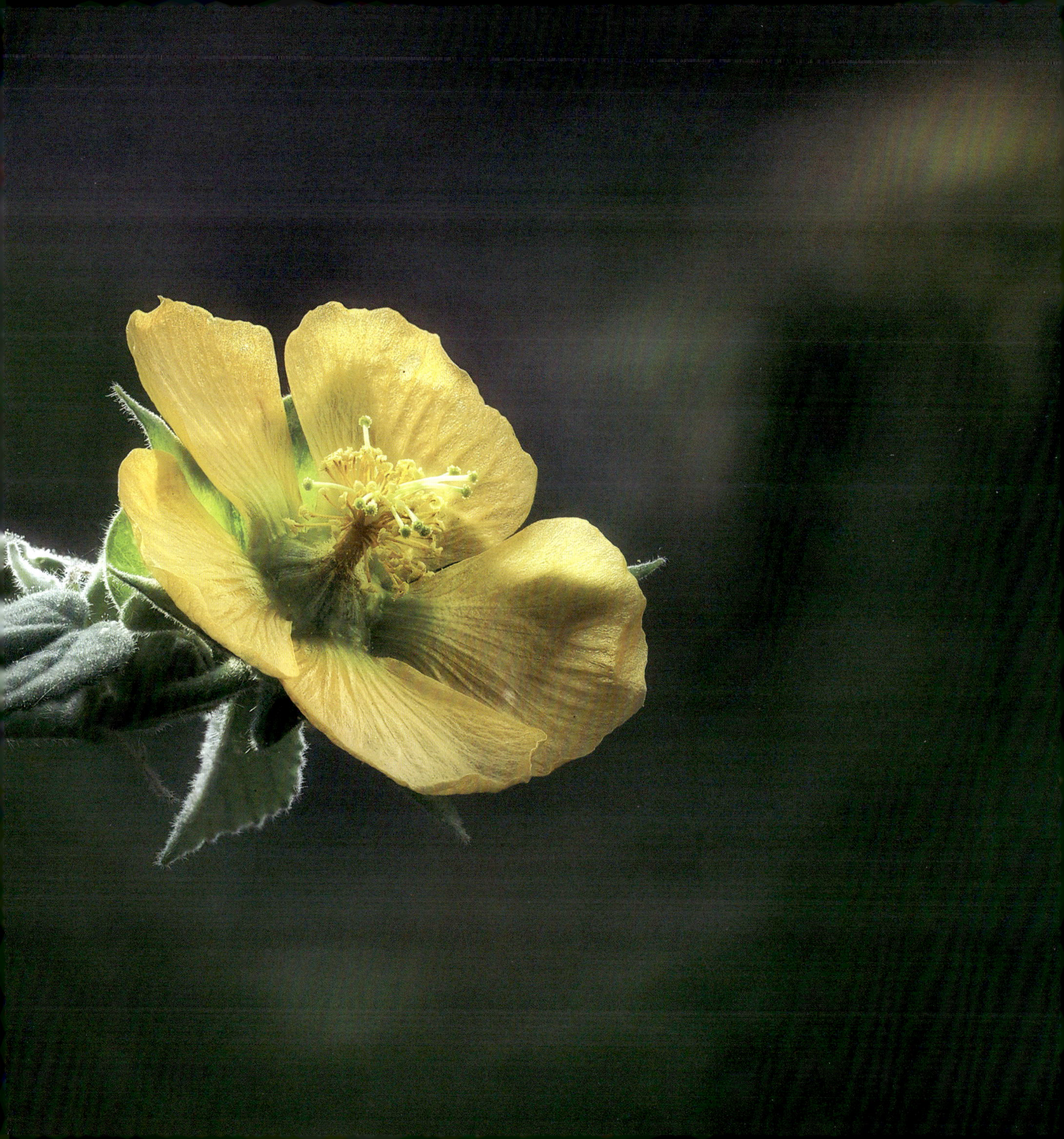

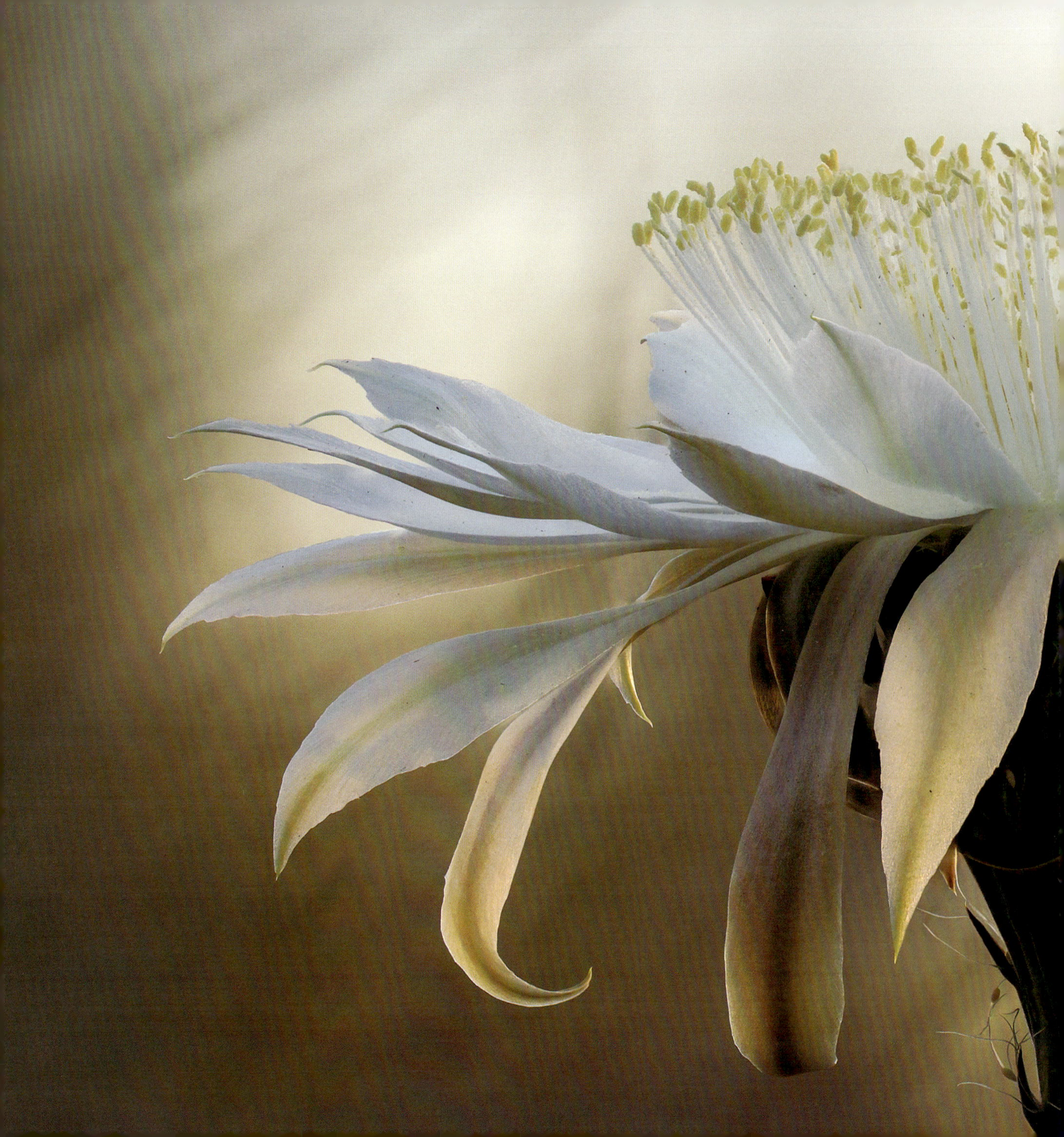

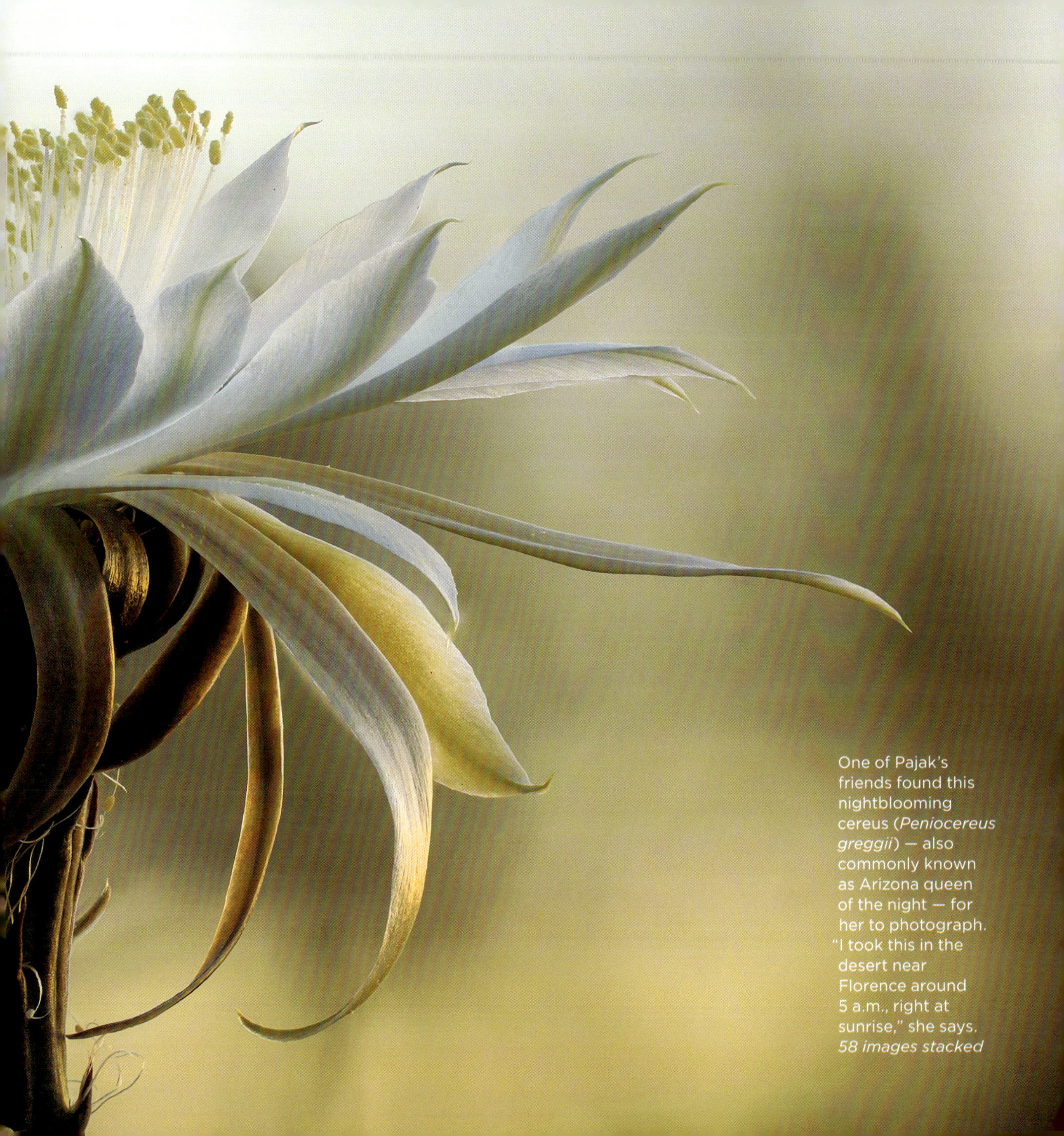

One of Pajak's friends found this nightblooming cereus (*Peniocereus greggii*) — also commonly known as Arizona queen of the night — for her to photograph. "I took this in the desert near Florence around 5 a.m., right at sunrise," she says. *58 images stacked*

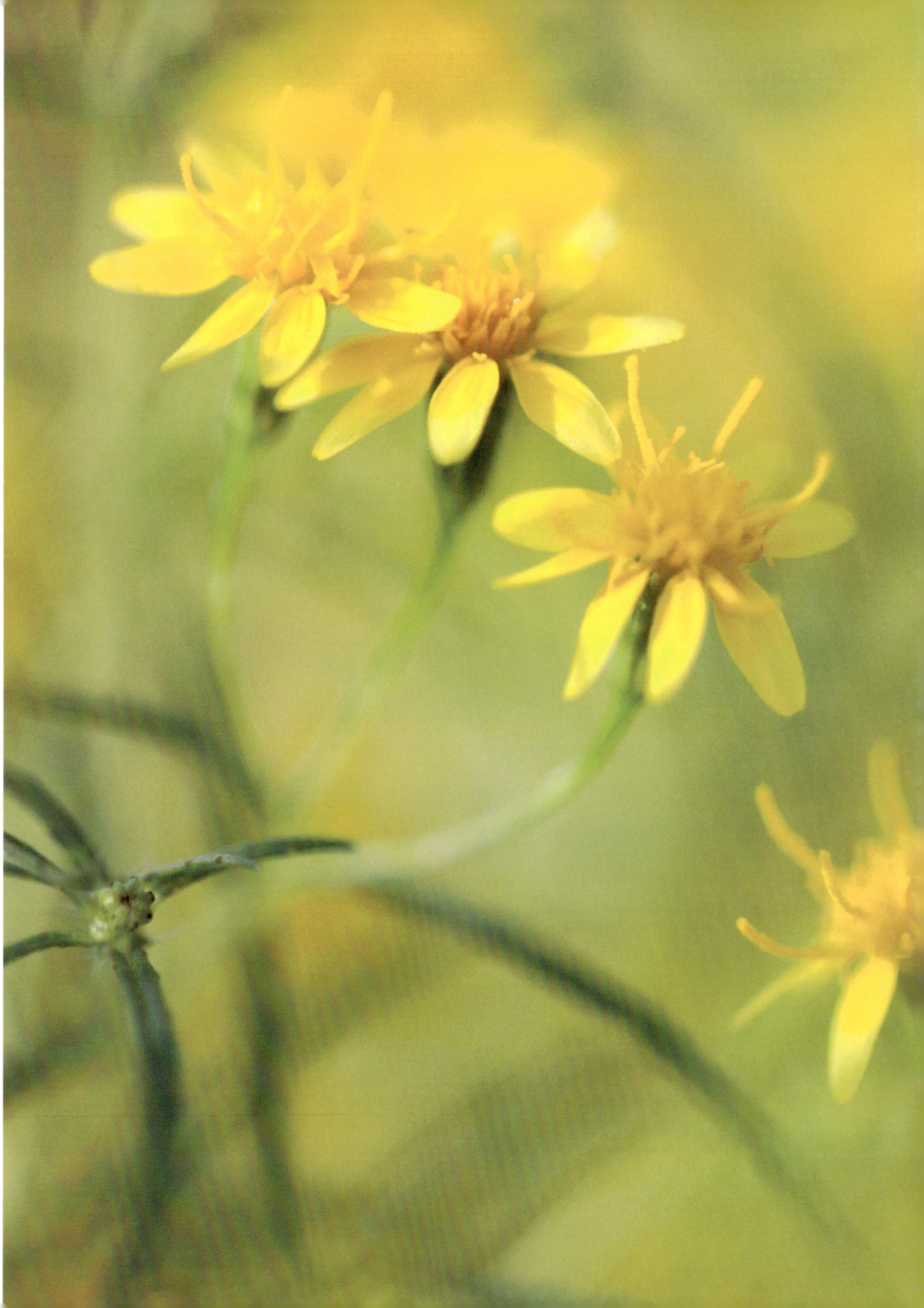

Although lovely to look at, cinchweeds (*Pectis papposa*) emit a rather overpowering odor. "There can be big masses of them, and I'll lie in them for hours to make photographs," Pajak says. "I end up smelling like the cinchweeds, too." *No focus-stacking*

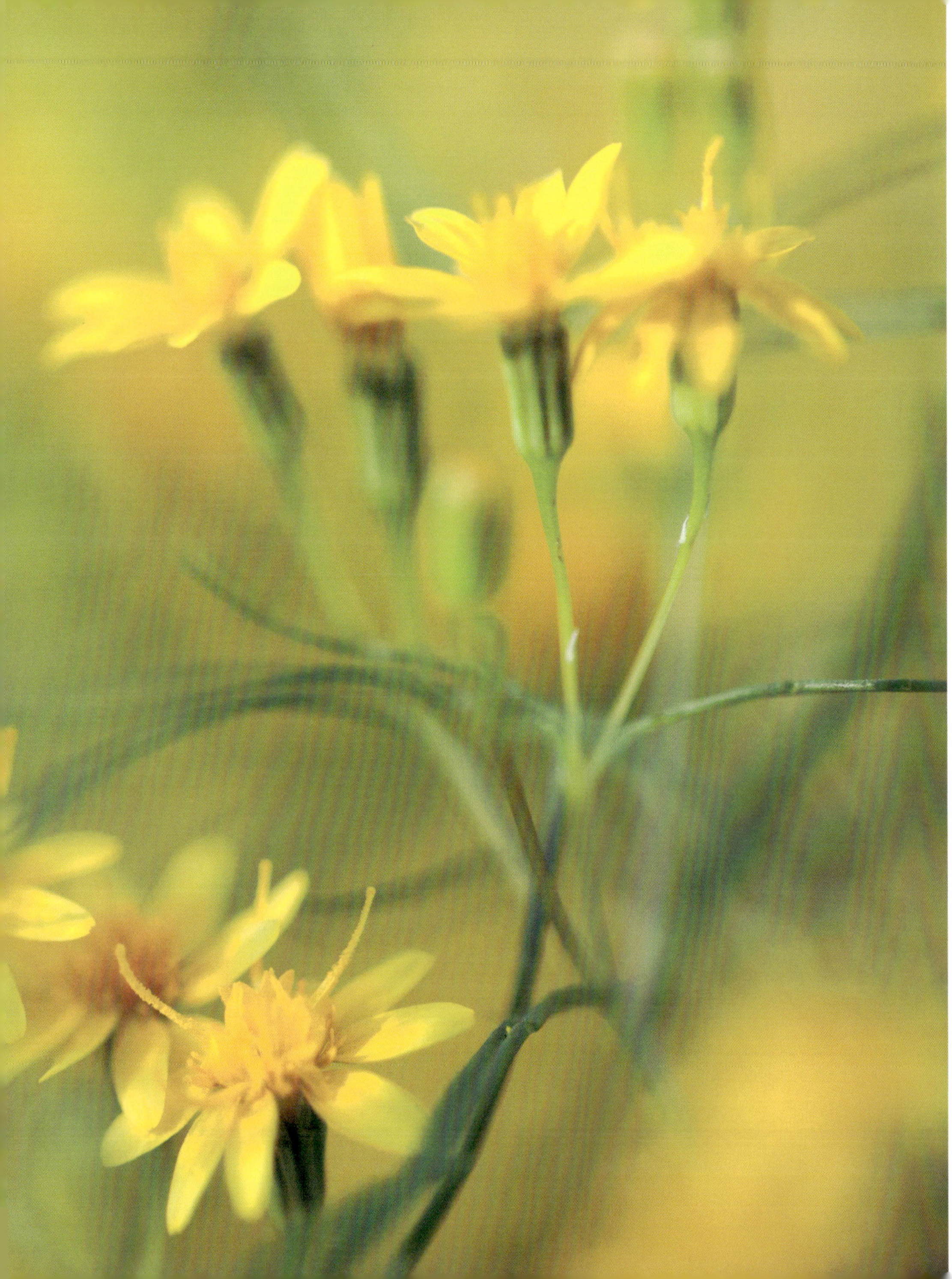

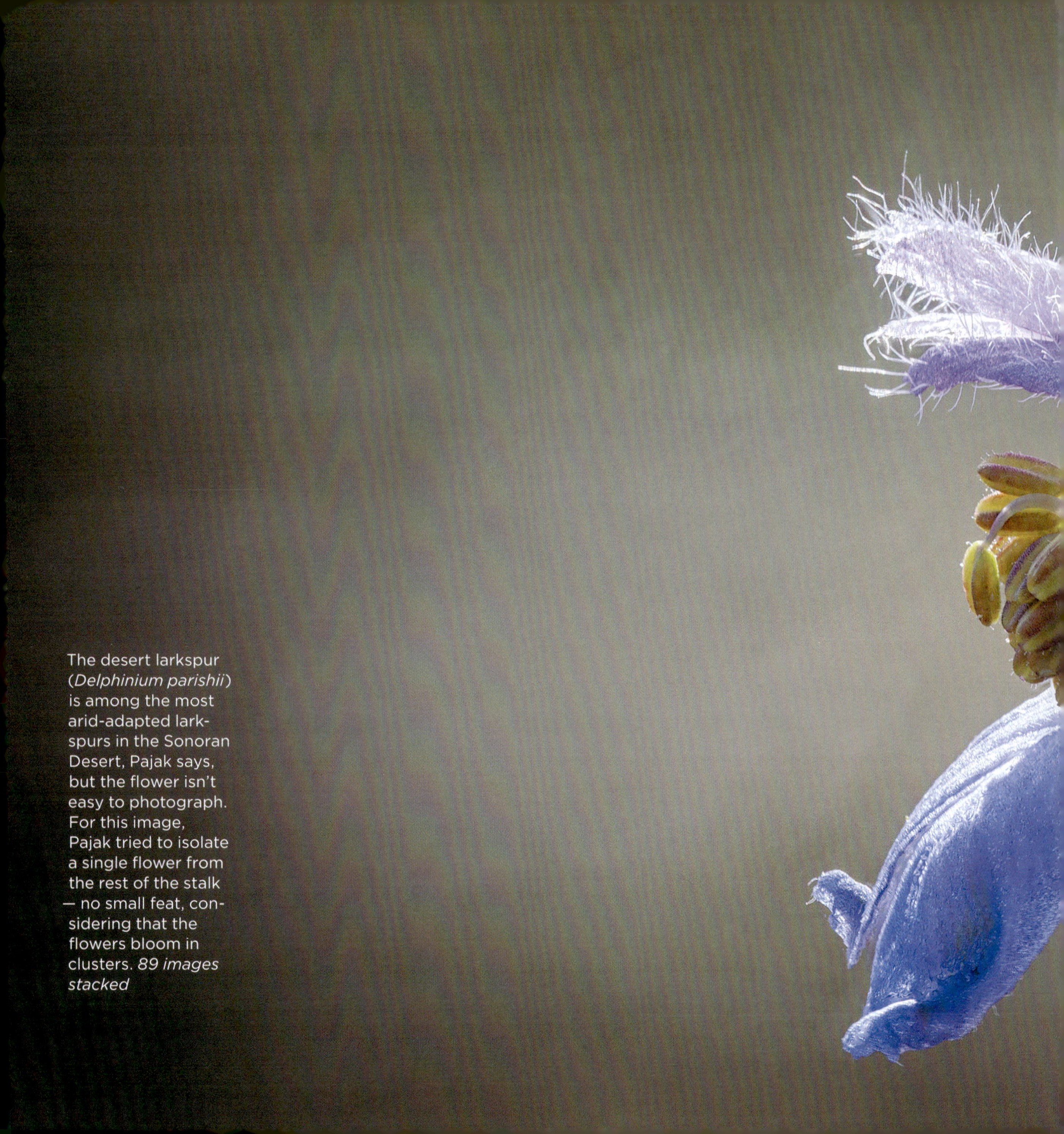

The desert larkspur (*Delphinium parishii*) is among the most arid-adapted larkspurs in the Sonoran Desert, Pajak says, but the flower isn't easy to photograph. For this image, Pajak tried to isolate a single flower from the rest of the stalk — no small feat, considering that the flowers bloom in clusters. *89 images stacked*

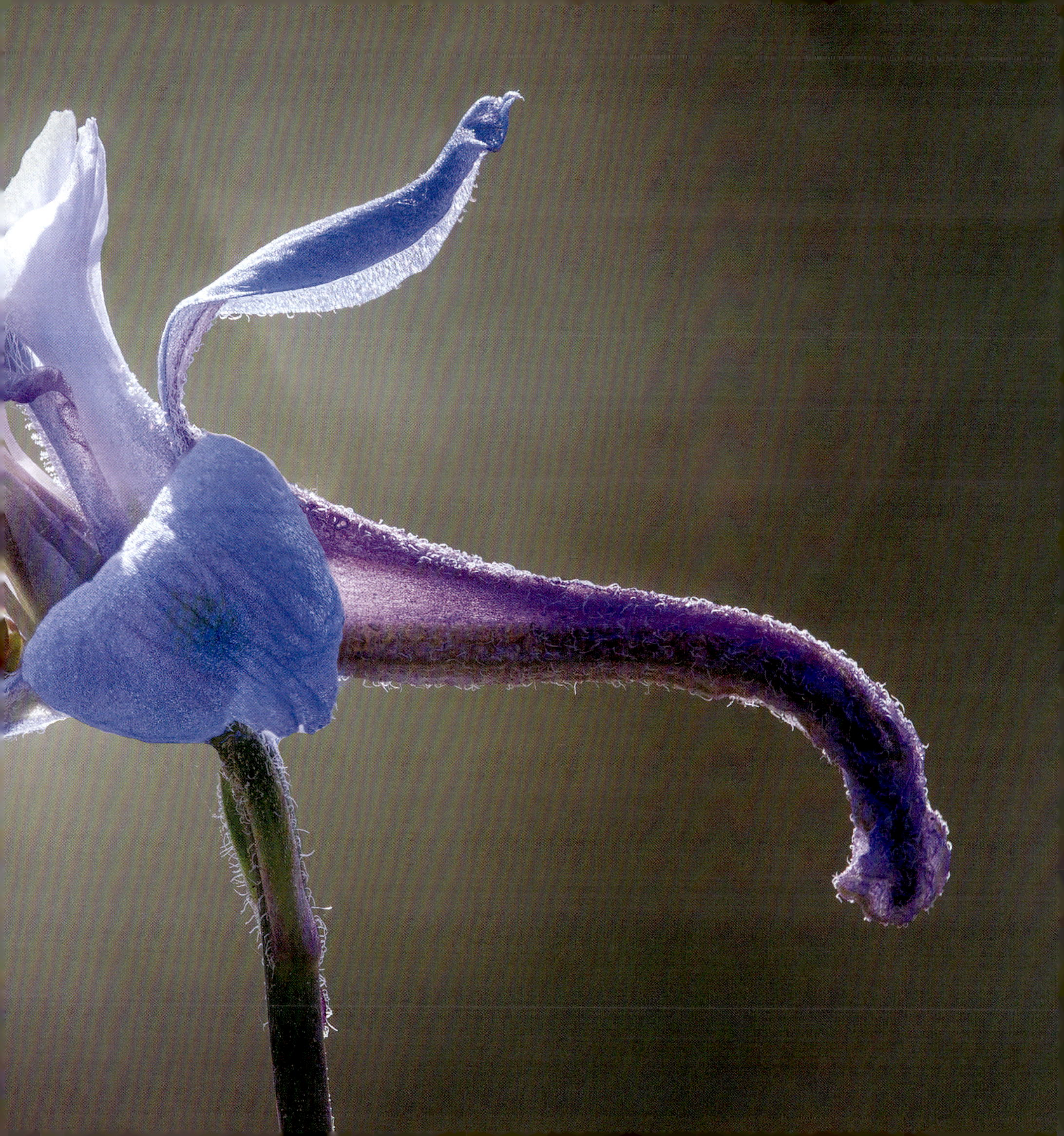

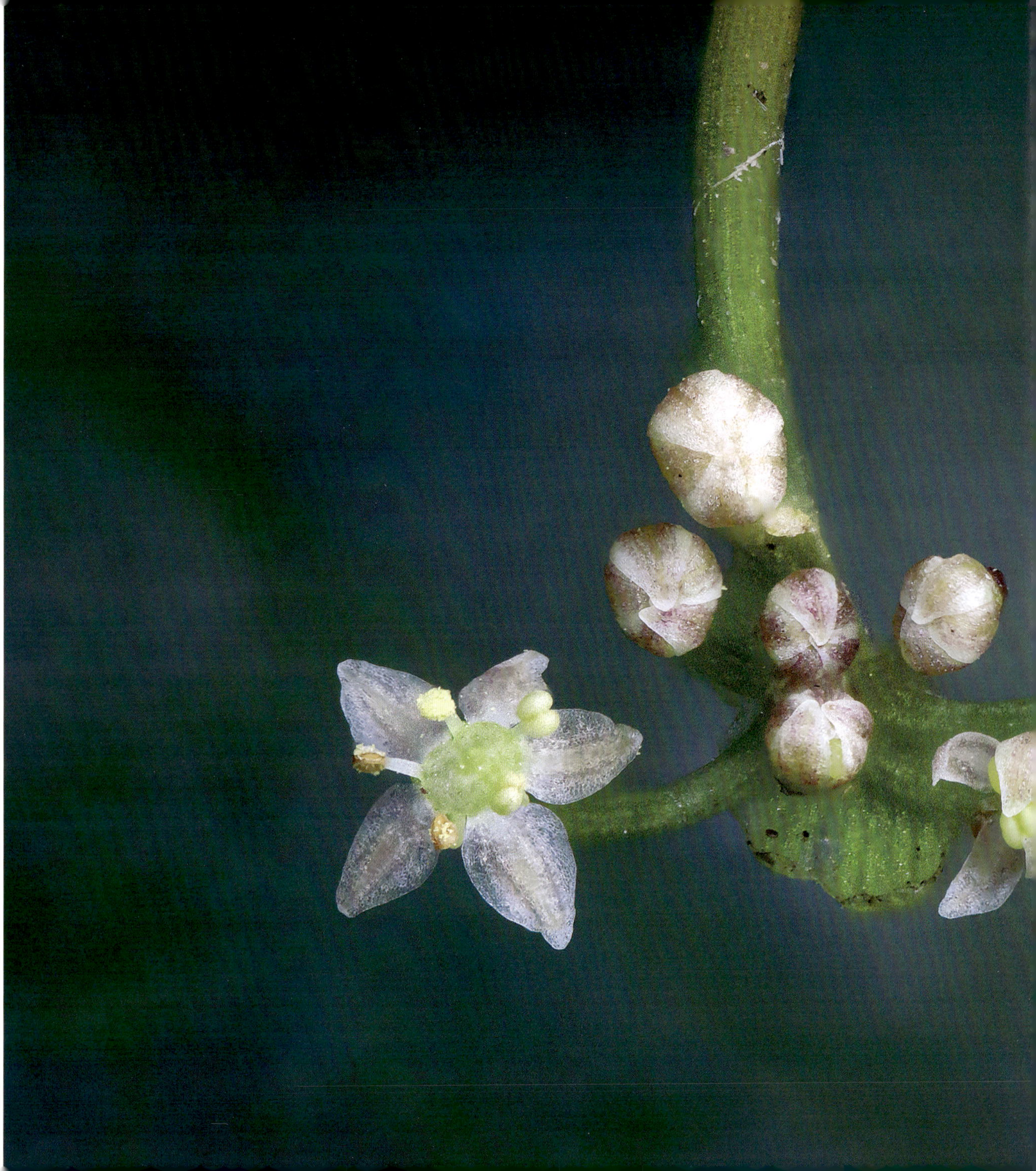

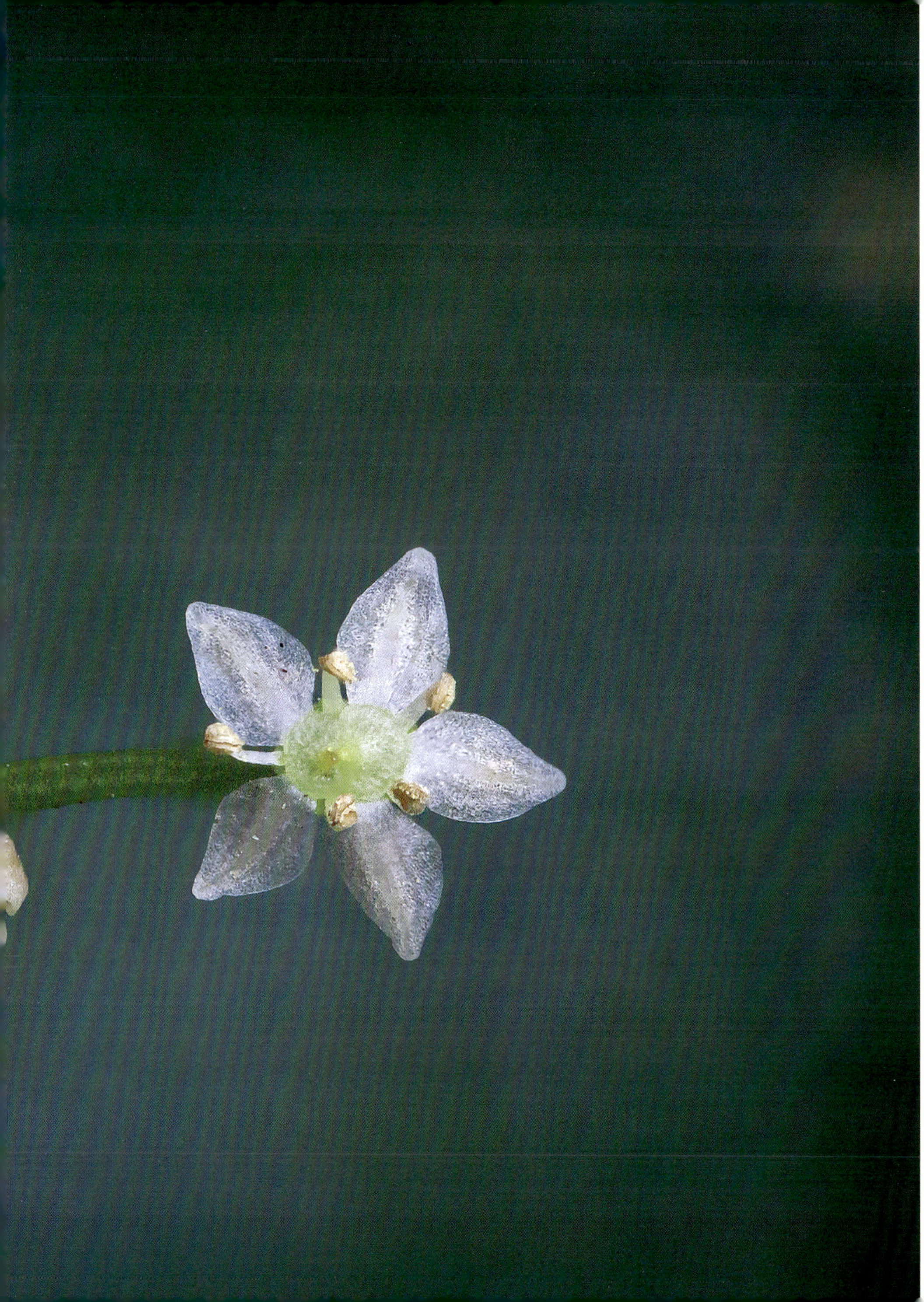

The Huachuca water umbel (*Lilaeopsis schaffneriana recurva*) is an important indicator of wetland health. But it's also incredibly rare and very hard to find. Pajak photographed this one within Las Cienegas National Conservation Area, near Sonoita. "This plant is so tiny, but I knew from botanists exactly where it was and where to look," she says. "So I went there and looked. And looked and looked and looked. There was nothing there. I saw the leaves, but no flowers. Then, I started combing through the grasses. I found them and spent a lot of time looking for one that I thought was in a pretty arrangement."
104 images stacked

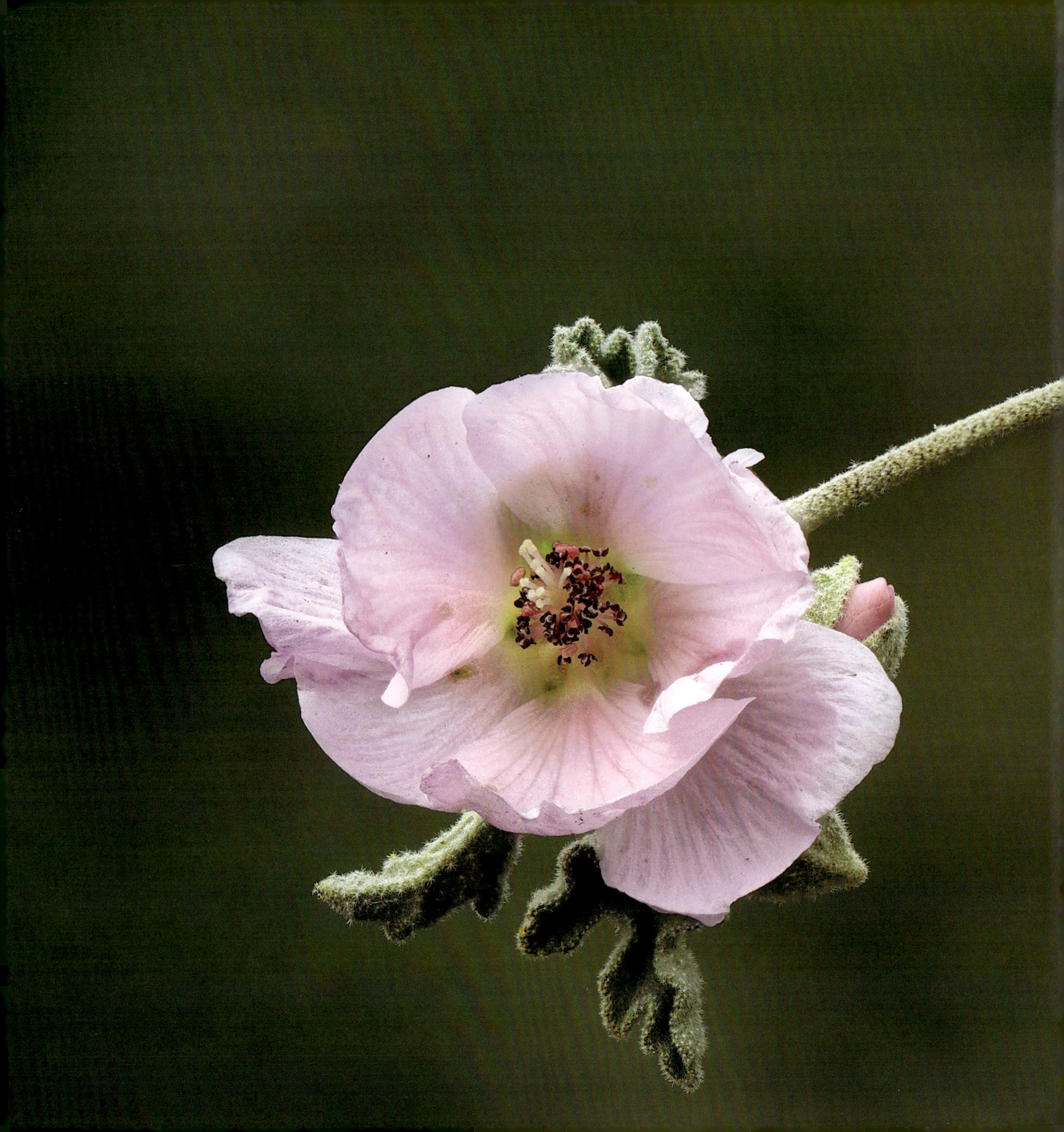

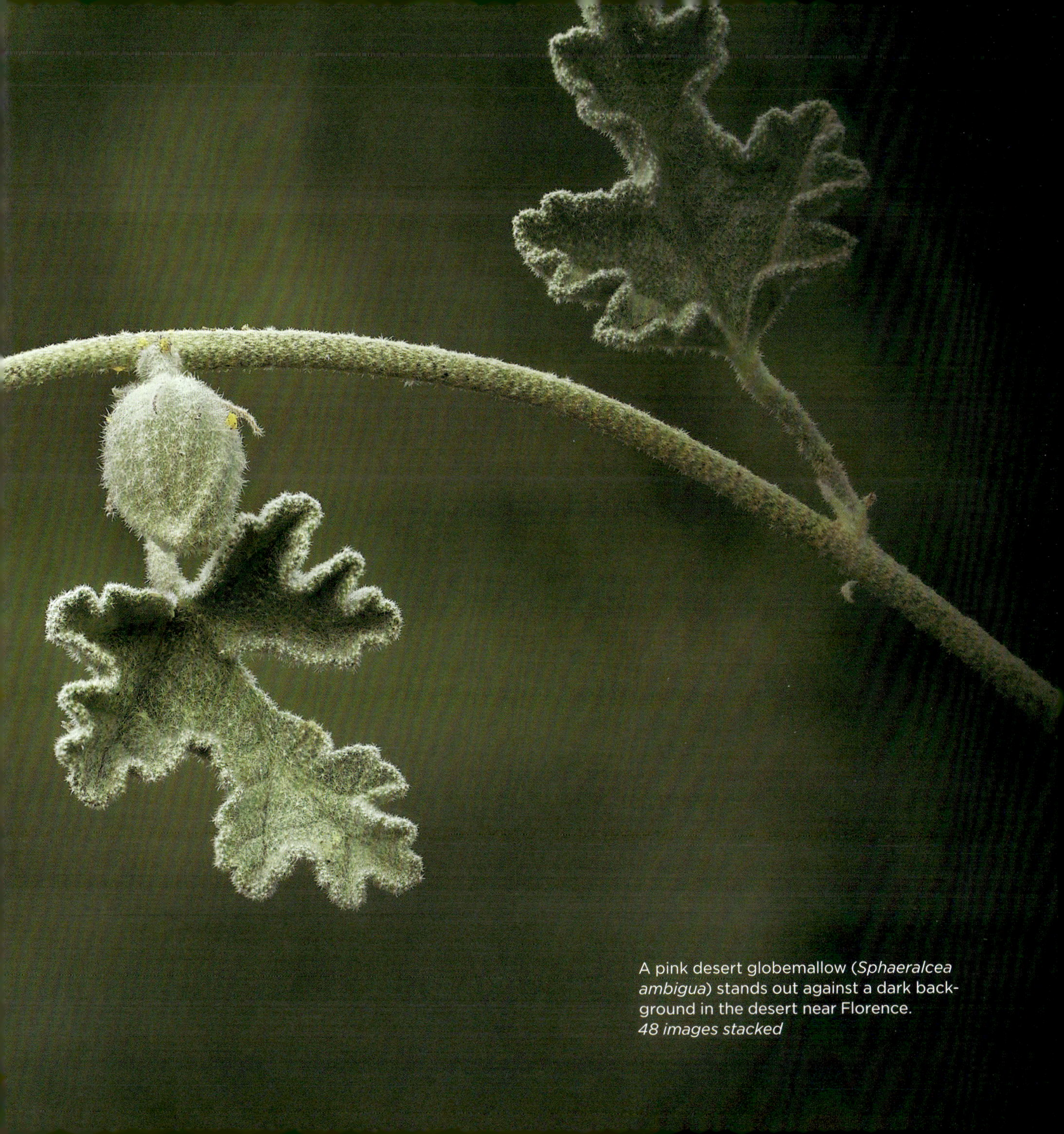

A pink desert globemallow (*Sphaeralcea ambigua*) stands out against a dark background in the desert near Florence.
48 images stacked

Pajak made this photograph of a tiny gilia (genus *Gilia*) when she first began focus-stacking. "It was growing on the side of the Florence-Kelvin Highway," she remembers. "It was so tiny, but it caught my eye, so I stopped to photograph it, even though I was heading somewhere else." *21 images stacked*

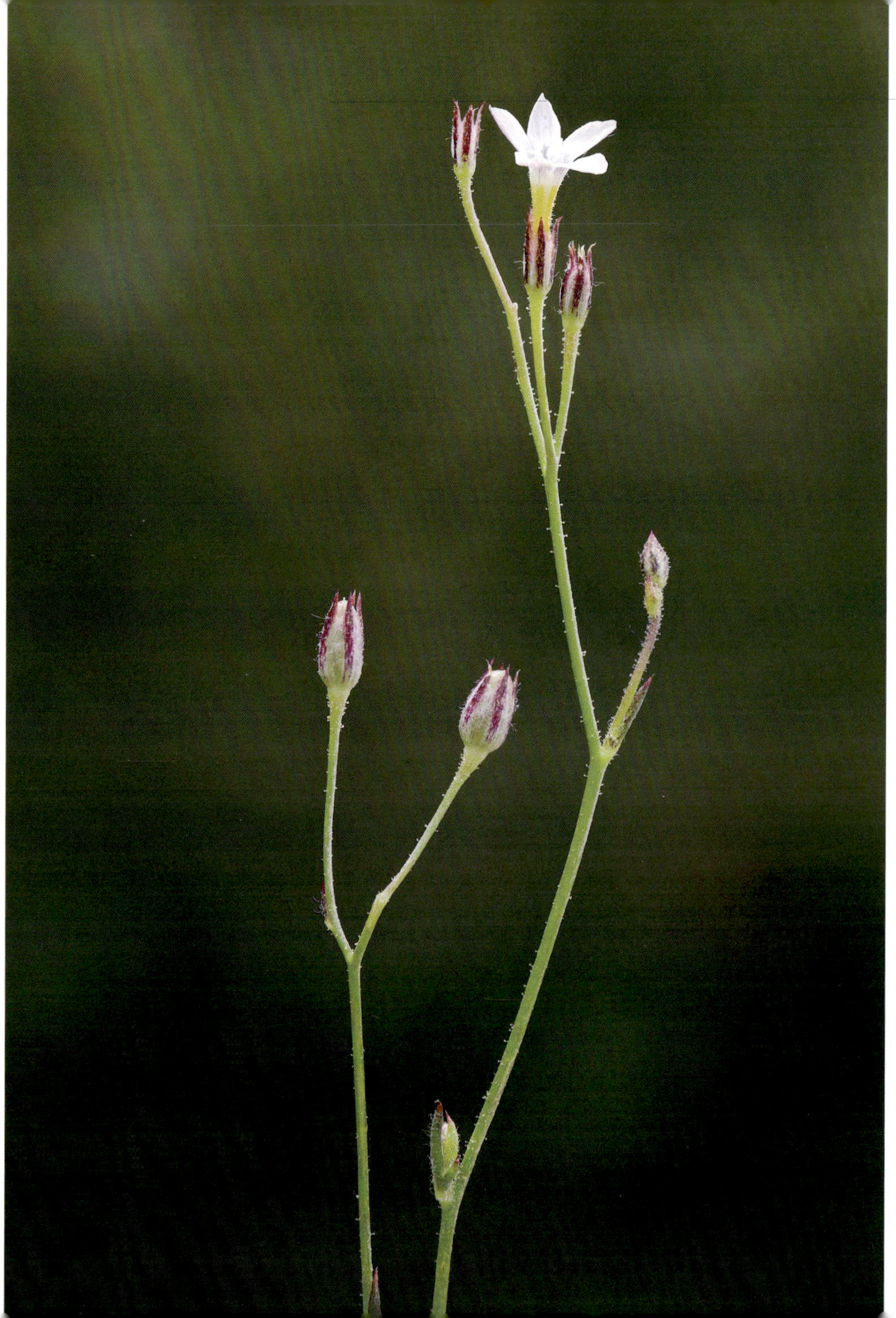

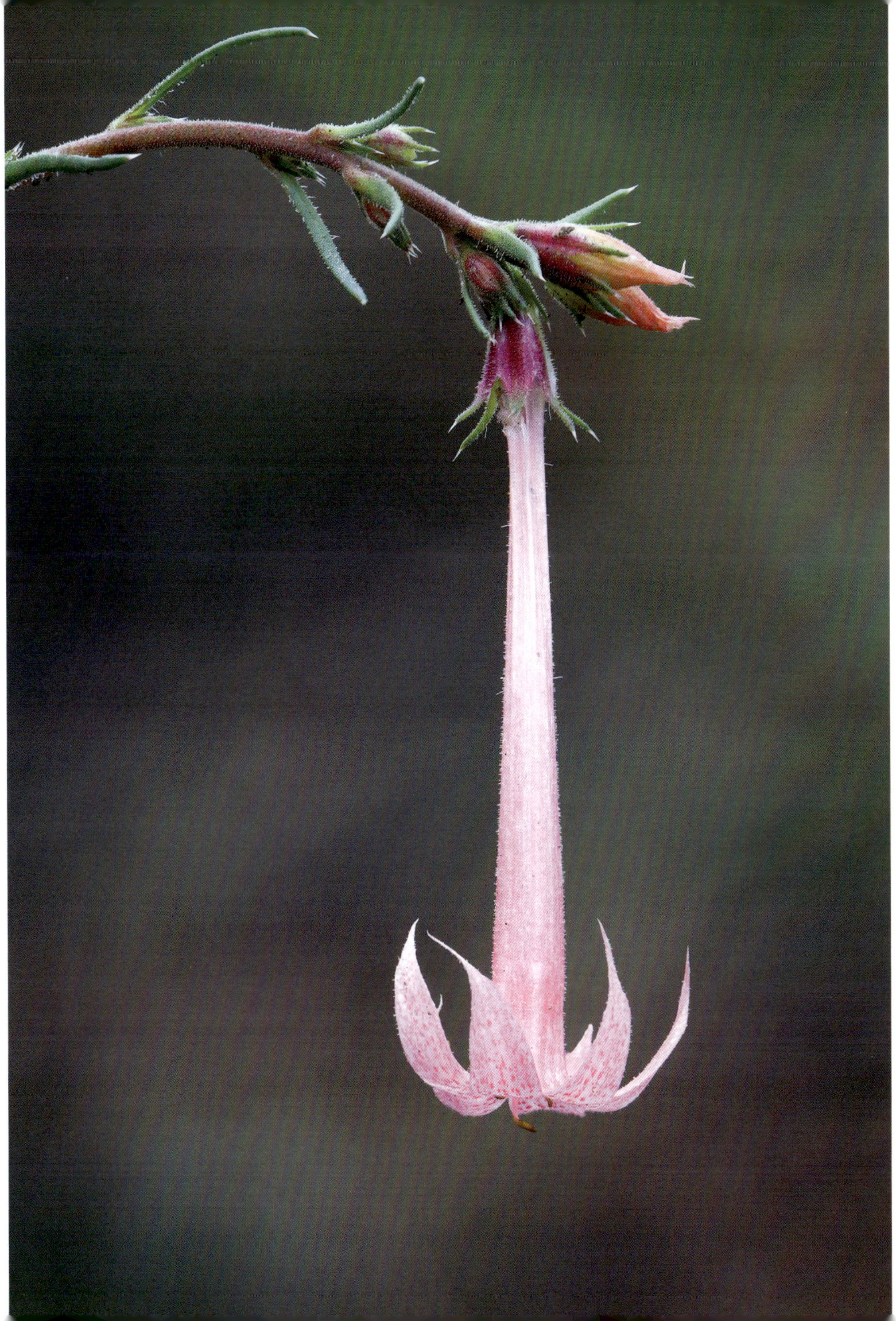

A slendertube sky-rocket (*Ipomopsis tenuituba*) grows in the Coconino National Forest northwest of Flagstaff. *29 images stacked*

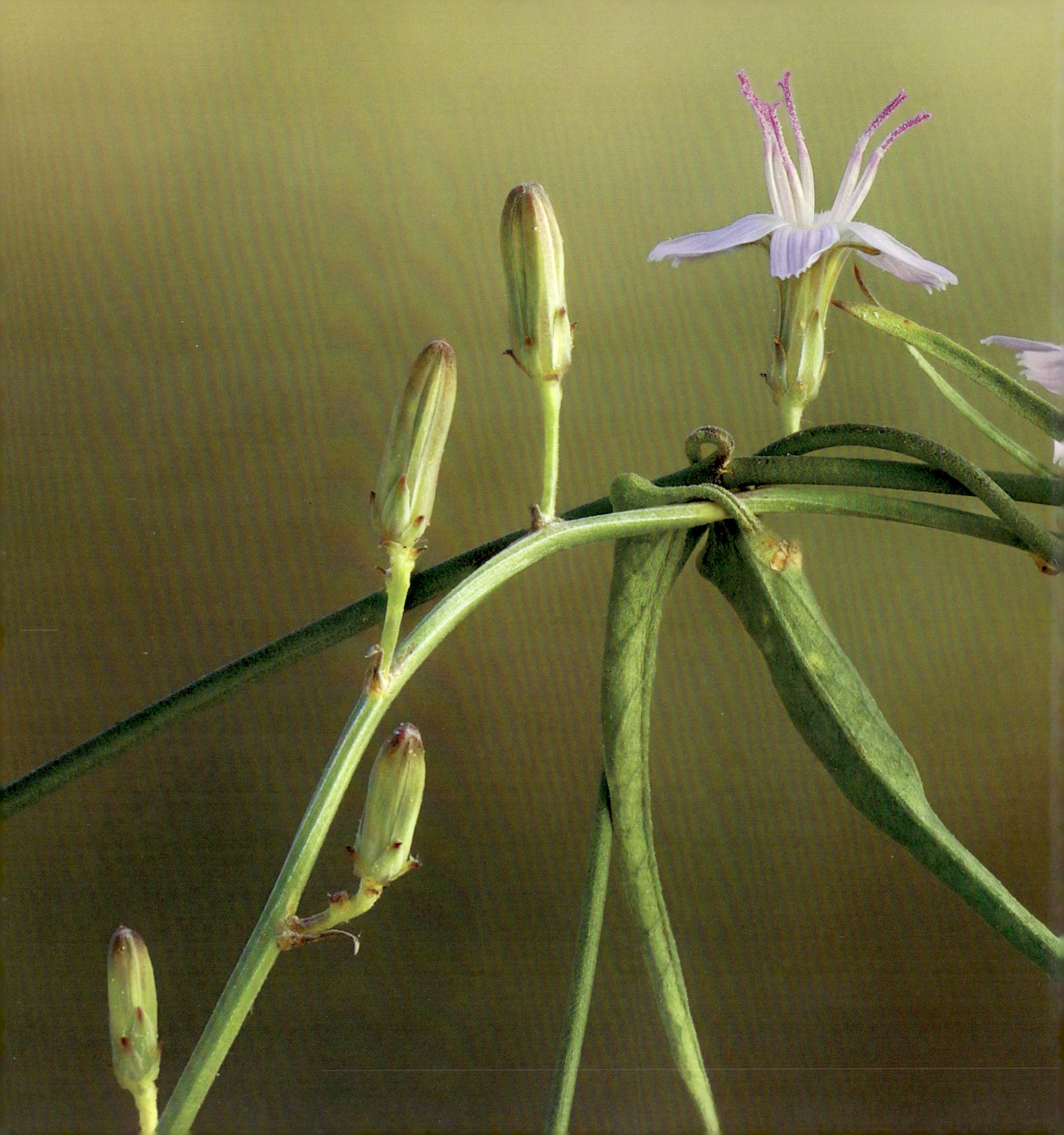

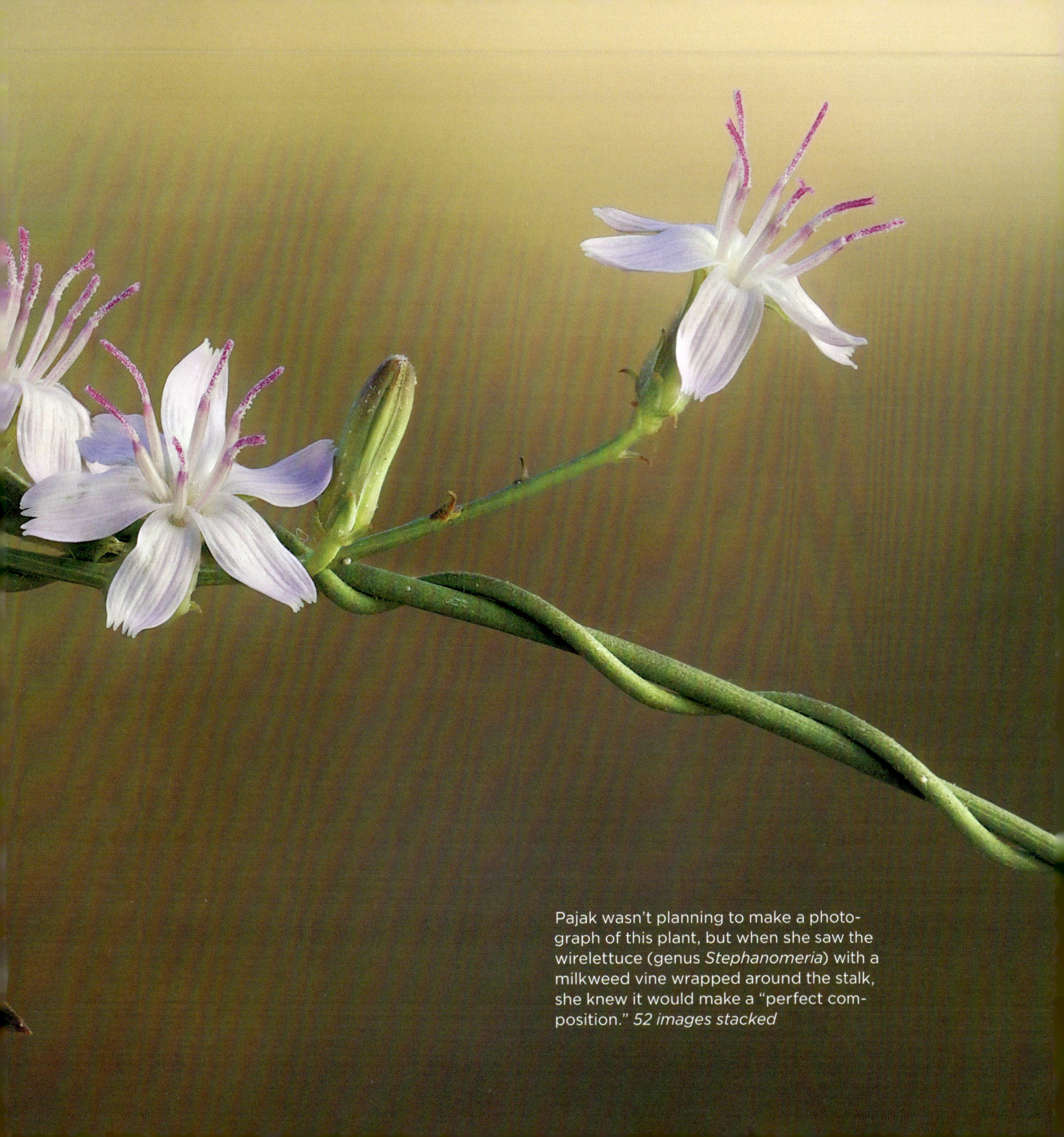

Pajak wasn't planning to make a photograph of this plant, but when she saw the wirelettuce (genus *Stephanomeria*) with a milkweed vine wrapped around the stalk, she knew it would make a "perfect composition." *52 images stacked*

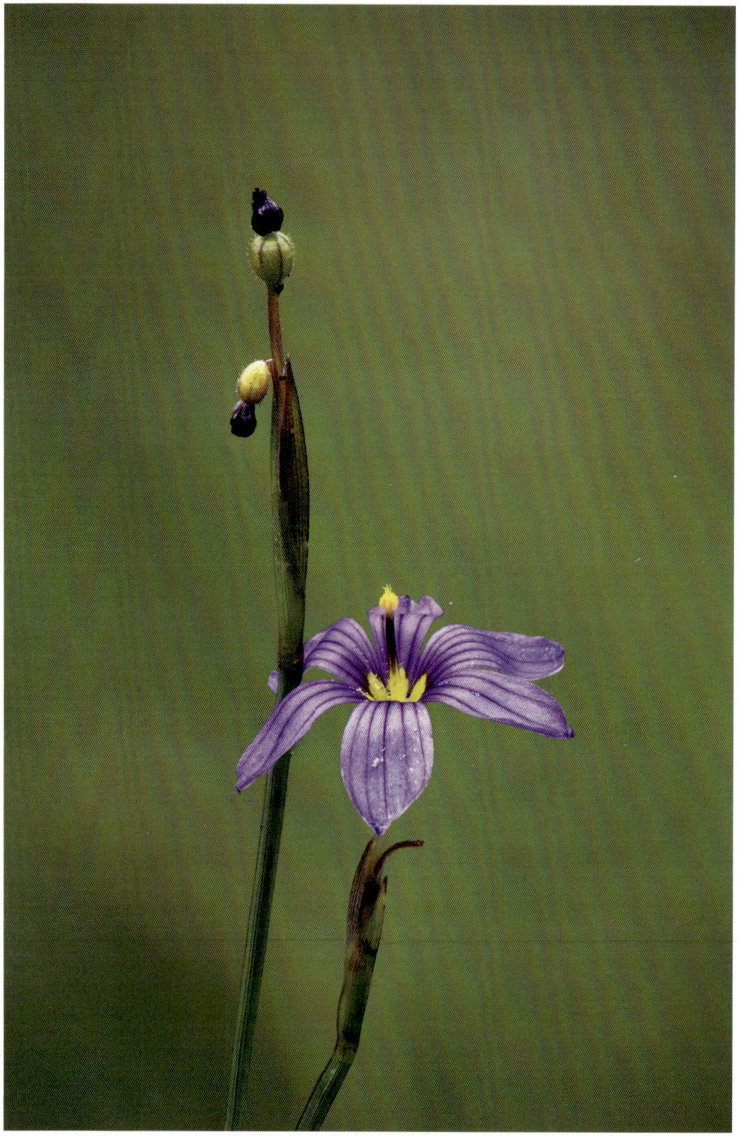

Stiff blue-eyed grass (*Sisyrinchium demissum*) grows in Lockett Meadow, near Flagstaff. *25 images stacked*